Praise for
My Charmed Life

"This memoir is filled with honesty, clarity and wit. Bernstein's writing is the most beautiful gem of all."

—Abby Sher, author of *Amen, Amen, Amen*

"Clever, funny and at times heartbreaking, *My Charmed Life* sparkles. Bernstein writes from the soul with insight and no-holds-barred honesty." —Valerie Frankel, author of *Four of a Kind*

"*My Charmed Life* is the *Love, Loss and What I Wore* for jewelry. This witty, romantic romp chronicles all the relationships in the author's life through the gems she was given from age five to fifty. Every page is frank, funny and completely relatable. A debut as dazzling as the vintage necklaces, bracelets and earrings Beth so vividly describes."

—Susan Shapiro, author of *Five Men Who Broke My Heart*

"This tender, funny, beautifully written memoir cleverly connects relationships both familial and romantic to the special gifts that found their way into Beth Bernstein's jewelry box and heart. As a nice Jewish girl with a severe jewelry jones myself, I empathized with every word of *My Charmed Life*—and envied Beth's collection and recollections. Safe to say this book is a gem." —Wendy Shanker, author of *Are You My Guru?*

"Beth Bernstein understands the complicated value of shiny, sparkly things. This book is about all they represent: our histories, loves and losses."

—Giulia Melucci, author of *I Loved, I Lost, I Made Spaghetti*

My Charmed Life

ROCKY ROMANCES,

PRECIOUS FAMILY CONNECTIONS

AND SEARCHING FOR A BAND OF GOLD

BETH BERNSTEIN

 NEW AMERICAN LIBRARY

NEW AMERICAN LIBRARY
Published by New American Library, a division of
Penguin Group (USA) Inc., 375 Hudson Street,
New York, New York 10014, USA
Penguin Group (Canada), 90 Eglinton Avenue East, Suite 700, Toronto,
Ontario M4P 2Y3, Canada (a division of Pearson Penguin Canada Inc.)
Penguin Books Ltd., 80 Strand, London WC2R 0RL, England
Penguin Ireland, 25 St. Stephen's Green, Dublin 2,
Ireland (a division of Penguin Books Ltd.)
Penguin Group (Australia), 250 Camberwell Road, Camberwell, Victoria 3124,
Australia (a division of Pearson Australia Group Pty. Ltd.)
Penguin Books India Pvt. Ltd., 11 Community Centre, Panchsheel Park,
New Delhi - 110 017, India
Penguin Group (NZ), 67 Apollo Drive, Rosedale, Auckland 0632,
New Zealand (a division of Pearson New Zealand Ltd.)
Penguin Books (South Africa) (Pty.) Ltd., 24 Sturdee Avenue,
Rosebank, Johannesburg 2196, South Africa

Penguin Books Ltd., Registered Offices:
80 Strand, London WC2R 0RL, England

First published by New American Library,
a division of Penguin Group (USA) Inc.

First Printing, July 2012
10 9 8 7 6 5 4 3 2 1

 REGISTERED TRADEMARK—MARCA REGISTRADA

LIBRARY OF CONGRESS CATALOGING-IN-PUBLICATION DATA:
Bernstein, Beth.
   My charmed life: rocky romances, precious family connections and searching for a band of
gold/Beth Bernstein.
     p. cm.
   ISBN 978-0-451-23693-7
   1. Bernstein, Beth. 2. Bernstein, Beth—Family. 3. Bernstein, Beth—Relations with men. 4.
Women jewelers—United States—Biography. 5. Women fashion designers—United States—Bi-
ography. 6. Jewelry—Design. I. Title.
   NK7398.B467A2 2012
   739.27092—dc23
   [B]   2012001052

Printed in the United States of America

PUBLISHER'S NOTE
While the author has made every effort to provide accurate telephone numbers, Internet ad-
dresses and other contact information at the time of publication, neither the publisher nor the
author assumes any responsibility for errors, or for changes that occur after publication. Further,
publisher does not have any control over and does not assume any responsibility for author or
third-party Web sites or their content.

*Penguin is committed to publishing works of quality and integrity. In that spirit, we are proud
to offer this book to our readers; however, the story, the experiences, and the words are the author's alone.*

In dedication

> *To the real gems in my life:*
> *My mother and best friend, Shirley Bernstein Bonazzo, for her unconditional belief in me, and who will forever be with me. And my grandmother Ida Botwinick, for her continuous and loving guidance, and for making life, always, a little more glamorous.*

Dates, names, and identifying characteristics of many of the people and places in the book have been changed or obscured to protect the innocent and less innocent, and so that all my longtime exes who have remained friends will continue to do so without asking me for free jewelry for their wives and/or significant others.

Contents

CONTENTS

*My
Charmed
Life*

The Missing Pieces

I HELD ON TO the plastic Ziploc bag, which contained my mother's discreet antique wedding band from my stepfather, a sleek art deco baguette diamond stickpin, a long strand of baroque pearls my grandmother gave to her, Victorian moonstone bracelets and a black onyx and rose cut diamond* locket, encasing photos of me and my two younger brothers when we were kids. This was what remained: platinum memories of a life as a wife, mother and daughter, thrown into a sandwich bag. I had looked at the jewelry as if

---

* Rose cut diamond: an early style of diamond cutting with a flat bottom and triangular facets that form a dome at the top. This cut was most prevalent in the sixteenth through eighteenth centuries and was said to have originated in India. Over the past ten years, new versions of these old cuts have witnessed a renewed popularity in all forms of jewelry in white and natural-colored diamonds.

it were foreign, belonging to and worn by someone I had never known or seen before, someone else's mother, not mine—not the woman who held me together, the woman whom I loved so deeply and admired for as long as I could remember, the woman whose possessions the nurse handed me while softly saying, "She's gone."

Sometime after my nightly eleven p.m. phone conversation with my mother, ending with her usual "Lock your door. I love you and I'm always here for you," and her getting dressed for work in the morning, she blacked out and went into a coma. Three hours after the ambulance rushed her to the hospital and the doctors started working on her in ICU, she died unexpectedly from a brain aneurysm. She was fifty-five and I was thirty-two, and nothing in my life after the moment I was given the jewelry she had been wearing would ever be the same. I had lost my confidante, my best friend and the person who was . . . home.

It was incomprehensible that I would never see her again. I had no time to prepare; not that I could have been ready to lose the woman who put my life back together every time I had my heart broken, who made friends for me when I was shy, and ate Mallomars with me when I was sad. My mother believed I could be anything I wanted, that I was intelligent and beautiful, even in my adolescence, while going through my awkward stage, with braces and a badly feathered haircut. She viewed any guy who dumped me as unworthy of me and "knew in [her] heart" that, when I was ready, I would find someone who would love me as much as she did.

I didn't know how long it would take me to grieve, when it would start, if it would ever stop. I didn't know then that it would turn into something deeper, a sense of loss, an emptiness that could never be plugged up, that would get more bearable with time but would never go away. There would forever be something missing—my reflection, the woman who looked back at me in the mirror and said, "No matter who you are, you're okay by me."

Always my style guru, she taught me the fun and highly coveted skills of figuring out the times of year when Bergdorf's was having a sale, how to make Calvin Klein or Michael Kors clothes fit no matter what size they were and how to get a bargain at Saks instead of rummaging through Loehmann's or other discount stores. This was so we could avoid communal dressing rooms with unforgiving lighting and women who were not past pilfering the pile you had spent a dizzying amount of time to accumulate.

When it came to jewelry, she quoted Coco Chanel: "Take one piece off before you leave the house." She taught me how to keep it simple—that fine pieces are meant to add a little sparkle while still allowing your personality to shine through; how to mix antique and modern, faux and real, and somehow make it all work. In the seventies, we would check our mood rings like we did the Magic 8 Ball, as if they were cheat sheets for our lives. These were the moments, the simple ones that I longed for most and still do, just as I still go to pick up the phone to call whenever something small or big happens or if I am just in need of my closest friend.

My mother had an eye for fashion and an innate sense of taste. I had the most fun dressing up next to her, first in her clothes as a young girl and then while helping each other get ready for an important meeting, date or her small, simple yet elegant second wedding to my stepfather, Manny, when I was eighteen.

My life changed forever when I lost her. But the lessons that she slipped in along the way eventually helped me to figure out who I was. I began to realize my passion for jewelry and the meaning and sentimentality attached to different keepsakes only when she passed away, how her jewelry, along with my own—the pieces handed down, given and not given to me as gifts—would eventually tell the story of my life and would shape my career. These memories and mementos will always be with me and have linked together my past and my present.

Each year when the anniversary of her death rolls around, I take out the pieces that were passed down to me. As I slip on her long strand of creamy baroque South Sea pearls with its engraved platinum clasp, I envision her reflection in the mirror and pretend I am standing next to her once again, a young girl, dressing up in her jewelry. I imagine her looking back at me, her eyes warming over with pride for the daughter who so wanted to emulate her, her smile filled with understanding. As I continue getting dressed, I slip on her moonstone bangles—"three for luck" as she used to say—and hope she knows that it's her voice I always hear whenever I need courage, strength or a good laugh.

With the baguette stickpin I fasten a black cashmere sweater that has lost a button. And when I feel her eternal presence beside me, I hope I am reflecting the woman she would have wanted me to become.

CHAPTER I

Hoop Earrings

B Y THE TIME I was five, I was convinced I knew my personal style best and began choosing my own clothes and jewelry (or at least my mother allowed me to believe so). I wore only skirts or dresses and accessorized with abandon, borrowing an armful of my mother's frosted and clear Lucite or wood bangles for a dash of color, although they rarely left the house with me. The bracelets were too big for my wrists and they would fall to the floor, where I would leave them in favor of colorful candy necklaces that were a timeless and versatile jewelry item—they went with all the pastel clothes I owned.

I believed wholeheartedly in the transformative power of jewelry—how it made me feel more regal and glamorous, changing me from a shy, ordinary girl into a shimmering princess from a faraway land. Although I wasn't quite sure exactly how to express these thoughts back then, I knew that I felt prettier, more outgoing and more grown-up when I put on a long enamel daisy pendant with purplish petals and a yellow center and saw the way it brightened up a white turtleneck and brought out the various hues in a multicolored striped miniskirt. The diamanté ropes of chain that were designed as belts, which I wore instead as sashes, completely popped when draped across a simple jumper dress. Like most young girls, I subscribed to the "more is more" philosophy of how many five-and-dime, mix-and-match pieces I could pile on.

When I turned seven and was in second grade, my mother was completely overwhelmed by caring for my two younger brothers. As long as I wasn't wearing angora in summer or open-toed sandals in winter, and there were no visible Kool-Aid stains, I had free rein over my wardrobe choices.

Each night I carefully laid out my clothes for school. I still refused to wear pants, and I loved anything that made either a bold or glittery statement. I wore miniskirts with cotton turtlenecks, simple shift dresses and my favorite, a Marlo Thomas *That Girl* swing-style coat. I never left the house without my very own bracelets—plastic see-through, slide-on bangles with sparkles that swished around inside them—and my new favorite item, earrings.

"Come closer. You have a horrible rash on your ear. Let me have a look before you leave for school," my mother said to me as she tried to get a spoonful of mashed pears into my brother David's mouth. He spit it out at her. Prior to that moment, I had been able to go unnoticed for about a week. My mother had been busy with David, an infant, and Eric, four years old, whom my grandmother had renamed "the Terror." He was in his superhero phase, and his trick of the moment was to tie a ratty towel around himself like a cape and try to leap from tall staircases. Other times he would lock himself in the bathroom and try to make his Batmobile escape. He was, as the entire family referred to him, "a handful."

When I wasn't trying to keep Eric from his other hobbies—falling into the lake or climbing up the counter to the top of the refrigerator—I helped my mother with David, offering my services primarily because I had felt guilty about my reply when my father called me from the hospital to tell me I had a baby brother. I had demanded that he be given back. "I already have one of those. Bring me a sister instead," I said in a tone not unlike the Wicked Witch of the West. Once David was home, I got into my role as eldest sibling, showering him with love and relishing the fact that, unlike Eric, he did not yet have the dexterity with which to snap off my dolls' heads.

Despite the bratty and unladylike way in which I had handled my younger brother's arrival into the world, I definitely was a girly girl. That morning, when my mother finally noticed my ears, she said again, "Honey, please come closer. I might need to call Dr. Reller." I hated our pediatrician, although he had probably saved my life when my appendix was about to burst a year earlier. But I was convinced that he never forgave me for kicking him in the face when I woke up in the hospital and he wouldn't take the IV out of my arm. To even the score, he gave me a shot for everything from a stubbed toe to a runny nose.

"It's not a rash. They are my new posts," I said, disappointed that my mother could not distinguish my creative cutout flower earrings from hives.

Upon closer inspection, she said, "You can't go to school with bits of pinkish red paper taped to your ears. Your teachers will think I am nuts for letting you out of the house like this."

"Then let me get my ears pierced. Or they might really talk about you when you go on parent-teacher night." At age seven, I was just starting to assert my independence. In addition to being a tad precocious, I saw how my mother and grandmother interacted when they were trying to make their points with each other. Most of the time humor or a little hint of sarcasm was involved.

"When you are old enough to drive."

"What do the two have to do with each other?" I asked.

"They both occur around the age of seventeen."

"I need a better reason."

"Okay. Here you go." She was exasperated. "I am your mother and you will listen to me."

"Why?"

I loved confronting her when I suspected she didn't have a rational explanation. My father told me I would probably make a good lawyer one day, as I was adept at pleading my case. My mom called it "hocking someone into getting what [I] wanted." Either way you looked at it, it wasn't working.

"If you want to look ridiculous, then go. You'll be late. But tomorrow you are leaving with clean ears."

I bit my lip hard to fight the tears. The thought of looking "ridiculous" was enough to send me into a panic. Although I could talk to my mother and my maternal grandmother about everything—Nana Ida called me her little chatterbox—I had a problem relating to girls my own age. It wasn't that I lacked things to say. It was more as though every time I tried to talk, I'd push back down the words that might come out to make me sound like a complete, but well-dressed, nerd.

Moving from nursery to kindergarten to elementary school didn't help. Just as I had settled in and felt more at ease in the lunchroom or playground, it would be time to change again—different kids, teachers and classrooms. I never liked being thrown into a new situation. I still don't.

During the summers, my family rented a small bungalow

in Monticello. It was a community of cottages that had only the barest essentials but were situated on beautiful grounds with a lake to swim, canoe and kayak, and constant activities for parents and kids. These months, when I was supposed to be having fun, were the most traumatic. All the girls were in cliques and were related somehow, first or second cousins. This was a form of nepotism I had never encountered in my hometown of Fresh Meadows, Queens, but one that I would quickly understand. They were popular amongst themselves and therefore with everyone else. This got them short-listed for the most fun activities by the pool, landed them partners for canoeing, offered line-cutting privileges at the canteen for ice cream and, worst of all, gave them a head start on our race for the boys on Sadie Hawkins Day.

To offset my shyness, and help me make friends, my mother threw themed slumber parties where we'd play dress up as our favorite characters from TV shows or Disney movies. Our last summer in Monticello, she made ten girls banana curls, fed us miniature-size pizzas, hamburgers, hot dogs and grilled cheese. She even whipped up tiny cupcakes in different flavors, almost forty years before it became a trend. We played all the newest board games she bought for that night, and danced to the latest Monkees and Tommy James and the Shondells albums. She taught us how to do the frug, the swim twist and generally move our hips in time with the music. My mother won the girls' hearts and a hell of a lot of friends for me with gift bags of confectionary treats that rivaled those of the best Halloweens. She also threw in an extra surprise of plastic cocktail rings or dia-manté barrettes. I came out of that summer more outgoing, with a newfound confidence that everything I said wasn't dumb, backed by my mother's guidance and successful swag.

When the school year started, I had made two best friends, Janie and Deena. Although I wanted Deena's straight blond hair and Janie's teeth, which appeared to have no over-bite and were not destined for braces like mine, my mother was still the person I admired most.

Except for her lack of dangly earrings.

My mom was always dressed in the newest fashions and accessories. It was the late 1960s, and once a year she would travel with my father on his business trips to Europe. They would stop in London, where she shopped for clothes and jewelry at Mary Quant and on Carnaby Street for the bold collar necklaces, the large cutout Lucite flowers and geometric-shaped metal bracelets I had borrowed. She as-pired to the styles of top model Jean Shrimpton in fashion spreads and Julie Christie in the film *Darling*, and I aspired to look just like her.

Yet I was completely disheartened when I realized she was unaffected by earrings or the understanding of why I wanted them. I kept trying new techniques to get my ears pierced, mostly by asking (hocking) in different ways and at least once a week since the school year had begun. A place that had a huge sign in the window, EAR PIERCING INSIDE, had opened within walking distance from our apartment in Queens, between Bloomingdale's and Alexander's, where Janie had gotten hers done. I was excitedly telling my mother about it. "It's supposed to be quick and painless. I think you can just walk in without an appointment. When Nana Ida comes tomorrow, maybe she can take care of the boys while we walk over to check it out?"

She pulled me close. "When I was your age, I wanted certain things, but Nana Ida made the decisions. It was hard to accept at the time, but in the end I realized she was right. And please don't go running up the phone bills to call her to find out again if I was really once your age. You will have to take my word until she gets here tomorrow."

When I moped, my mother tried scare tactics. "There are things to be concerned about." In my mother's worldview, there was always something to worry about. Not that I didn't give her reasons during the first few years of my life. I got mumps and the German measles six months apart from each other. I had my tonsils and adenoids out at five, my appendix out when I was six and at seven a reaction to Benadryl, which she gave me for a small rash that turned into a visit to the emergency room for an even larger allergy to the medicine supposed to help cure the rash. I went into anaphylactic shock from a bee sting. From then on, she took me to the doctor every time I sneezed. But I still had to ask, "If I'm not scared, why should you be?"

She gave me a laundry list of reasons that included but

were not exclusive to infections—from mild to those on par with leprosy—holes coming out lopsided, hating them once I got them, looking more sophisticated than my second-grade years (I had no problem with that), and an exaggeration that the ears of my paternal grandmother, Nana Annie, were pulled down to her chin from wearing heavy earrings.

And then she went for it. "You've got beautiful dark hair, blue eyes and high cheekbones, but you come from a gene pool with women who have been cursed with humongous ears, not to mention thick lobes." She pinched mine. I looked carefully at hers, envisioned Nana Ida and Fanny, my great-grandmother, and realized she was right. My mother looked like Nana Fanny. Both had small graceful noses, full, perfectly shaped lips and large eyes. But if you thought about it, as I was now forced to do, their delicate faces were outsized by their large flappy ears. Nana Ida had less classically perfect features, yet she was attractive and could turn heads with a face full of character, with animated expressions and deep blue eyes. But she too had extremely large ears. And, yes, Nana Annie's were long. I had inherited the Dumbo-size ears from both sides of the family.

None of this mattered, though. I still wanted mine pierced like every other girl in my school. I started concocting a plan, which would eventually become known as the earring escapade or earring caper, depending on who would tell the story later in life.

BETH BERNSTEIN

It was something my mother had said about realizing that Nana Ida was always right that set my idea in motion.

The next morning, I created a mismatched pair of earrings, a star on the left and a half-moon on the right.

When I walked into the dining room, Nana Ida was already there, drinking her coffee and trying to get the cape off Eric before he had to leave for kindergarten.

"Come give me a big hug," she said, reaching out for me. As I leaned in, she squinted and asked, "What the heck are on your ears?"

"My new post earrings," I replied matter-of-factly.

"Ah," she said. "Well, let's see if we can fix the Scotch tape so it's not as noticeable." She went to work on my lobes. "Also, maybe they should be a little higher up." She leaned back, grabbed her glasses and took a closer look.

"Please don't indulge this, Ma," my mother said to my grandmother. "I told her yesterday was the last day she could go to school accessorized in Scotch tape."

"Well, at least we can make them look a bit neater." While my mother worried about germs and rare diseases, my grandmother was more concerned with anything looking out of place.

Outtakes of their conversations went like this:

MY MOTHER: "What do you mean, someone threw a fistful of sand in Beth's mouth? The kids put their dirty hands in that sandbox."

NANA IDA: "No one ever got sick from eating a little dirt."

MY MOTHER (not the least bit ironically): "If you must take her on the subway, sit far away from strangers."

NANA IDA: "Okay. We'd better make friends quickly with the other commuters then."

MY MOTHER (before they had hand sanitizers): "Please find a place to wash her hands after you get out at your stop."

NANA IDA: "Do you think the teachers who oversee the two hundred some-odd elementary school kids make them wash their hands every time they pick their nose and hold on to the seesaw?"

MY MOTHER: "That was something I didn't need to visualize."

Nana Ida then pushed the hair off my mother's face. "I had a seven-year-old daughter once, and it seems *you* lived to tell many tales." Loosening my mother up with her light-hearted approach, she asked, "Why don't you just let Beth do this already? She has wanted it for more than a year. All the young girls I see have them, and it's really a very safe procedure that takes about two minutes. Just because you were scared and chose not to get your ears pierced doesn't mean she should have to wait."

"I wasn't scared. I just never liked earrings."

Somehow the hankering for a little sparkle around the face skipped a generation in my mother.

But both Nana Fanny and Ida had their ears pierced when they were even younger than I was.

"That was a cultural thing," my mom said when I reminded her of that.

Nana Fanny wore Russian-style rose gold and diamond earrings that her mother gave her. She took the diamonds out of the settings and hid them with relatives on their way over from Russia. Those and her wedding ring were the only family heirlooms she brought. The earrings were rose gold with silver tops that made the imperfectly colored European cut diamonds gleam from the oxidized framed bezel. They were small and delicate and looked beautiful even on her big ears. Nana Ida wore larger styles that rested on the lobe in coral and mabe pearl. She was fifty-three when I was seven; she said she needed to hide the way her ears had started drooping, and it was important to camouflage what gravity had started taking down. (This is a concept I've become totally familiar with in the past decade of my life.)

"When she is seventeen. End of discussion," my twenty-nine-year-old mother said.

I tried, Nana mouthed to me.

But I had already worked out the plan and was bursting to tell my grandmother. I knew I'd have to wait till I got home from school. It was simple. I had decided that the one person who could trump my mother's decision was . . . her mother.

It was an overthrow of the crown at its best, and the worst that could happen was that my grandmother would say no.

She didn't, of course. We set the "caper" in motion in my room that night. "I'm taking Beth back to my place in Brooklyn with me when I leave on Friday for the weekend. We can go see Nana Fanny and stop in the city at the Automat and FAO Schwartz, and I can pop into my favorite store on Fifth Avenue to try to find some decent shoes."

Papa Rubin came home from his job at the printing factory, and Nana Ida had dinner ready for him. He was surprised and beamed when he saw me. Nana didn't share our scheme with him. We both knew he would also be nervous about infection; he'd be skeptical about going against my mom's wishes and would worry about anything else he could think of. My mother was the female version of her father—all heart and raw anxiety. Nana Ida was the go-getter. When she put her mind to something, it happened. If she was concerned about something, she kept it to herself and went about taking care of everything and everyone. The dynamic worked.

Ever since my grandparents met at a dance, Papa Rubin told Nana Ida almost every night that he married the most beautiful woman, complimented her on what a great cook she was—how her matzo balls were as light as air (they lay heavy in everyone else's stomach)—and he talked often about how he loved his "little ladies": Nana, my mom and me. The only regret I had about the whole scheme was that Nana had to lie to Papa Rubin. I asked her about how she felt fibbing to him. "It's for a good cause. He'll understand." And then she squeezed me tight.

I could hardly sleep in anticipation of the big day. What I really wanted were small hoop earrings in gold. I'd experimented with remodeling paper clips into circular forms and then forcing them tightly to my ears, but they poked hard and eventually would slide off and the tape wouldn't adhere to them. I tried slivers of tinfoil that I'd fashioned into thin circles. Although these didn't pinch, they also didn't stick. After many other trials and errors, I came up with the cutout posts.

Nana Ida told me she was taking me to her friend Mike who had a jewelry store on Flatbush Avenue and that he pierced young girls' ears all the time as part of his service. She got much of her jewelry fixed at Mike's and sent her friends there for graduation gifts and anniversary presents.

We had square potato knishes and Dr. Brown's cream soda at our favorite deli; then we walked over to the store where Mike showed me the array of surgical steel studs that I would have to wear for the first six weeks.

"Such a long time?"

"Yes," said Mike. "Please don't change them before that if you want them to heal properly, and then you will be able to wear other types of earrings." I liked that he had friendly eyes and talked to Nana Ida about people they knew in common and his son who was going to college. Before we sat down, Nana Ida showed me another case and there were the twisted wire hoops in yellow gold, around the size of a nickel, that I'd been dreaming of wearing.

"We will take a pair of these, Mike, for when she can wear them." I was in heaven until I saw "the gun." I'd heard about it being a little scary to look at but that it did the job much quicker and with much less infection than a piercing needle, which took ice and time, a completely steady hand and a really good eye. That was what Janie's mother had said. I remembered it vividly.

"The gun measures the distance from the bottom of the earlobe to the center, so there will be no miscalculations of too high or too low or uneven." Mike was talking to Nana Ida, and the room started to spin. "Oh no, Mom is right. Let's forget this," I said, about to jump out of the seat.

My grandmother rubbed the top of my hand and told me to close my eyes and think about the blackout cake we bought for dessert, the cocker spaniel puppy I had been playing with in the pet store earlier and the beautiful wire hoops I'd soon be wearing. The next thing I knew, Mike was handing me a mirror, and while my ears were slightly red around the little balls, everything looked great.

Papa Rubin shook his head when he saw them, but when my grandmother pointed out, "Our granddaughter is still alive and eating fish sticks," all he could do was smile at me and say to her, "Okay, but you explain this!"

I had never heard my mother shout loudly at my grand-mother before.

"I am her mother. I make the decisions. How could you disregard everything I said? Now whenever we have a dis-agreement, she will think she can come to you to fix it."

It was the first time I'd ever seen Nana Ida look sad. She flinched at my mom's words.

I tried to tell my mother it was all my plan. But it didn't matter; Nana took the brunt of it. I got punished, of course, and had a small infection in my right lobe, but nothing that a few extra alcohol swabs and a few days without earrings didn't cure.

It was my first act of independence, my first true gift of love, and it was the first time I experienced the push and pull of mother/daughter relationships.

CHAPTER 2

Going Steady Ring

V ICTOR WAS MY first true love. I was mad about
him from first through fifth grade, an indication
that I did not give up easily on romance, nor did I
heed early warning signs. Victor looked like a six-year-old
version of Bobby Sherman, with shaggy brown hair and bluish green eyes and the most adorable bridge of freckles across
his nose. He wore corduroy bell-bottoms with flannel plaid
shirts or T-shirts in muted colors. I coordinated my outfits
in shades of my favorite color, purple: angora sweaters with
miniskirts; jumpers and shift dresses with little cardigans,
accessorized by brightly colored crochet beaded or enamel
flower pendants and mixed colored and metal bangles that
clanged every time I moved my arm. I had hoped my favorite outfit of a white turtleneck with a lavender A-line skirt,
accessorized by a smiley-face necklace and a white patent

leather belt with matching high go-go boots (very Nancy Sinatra) would seduce Victor into finally talking to me.

"Maybe you can try talking to Victor about Pee Wee League. I can't buy you a new outfit every day for school just because you want Victor to notice you," my mom said. Not only didn't he notice; he didn't even shoot straw wrappers at me or pull my hair when I wore it in a ponytail. It was the first lesson I'd learned about boys, and it was from some TV show—if a guy did annoying things to you, it meant he really liked you. Only later I learned that in real life, if a guy did these things, he might be passive-aggressive or might really want you to go away.

But back to Victor—he was busy playing on the jungle gym with Jimmy Angelo and being first grade milk monitor.

It was finally Mrs. Abrams, my teacher, who gave me my big break. "We need someone to help out Victor as milk monitor at recess." I raised my hand, bracelets clanging. I think I actually jumped out of my seat and waved my hand as though trying to flag a bus five blocks down the street. Considering that no one else even lifted an eyebrow, I was a shoo-in for the job. We had approximately two minutes to go to the fridge, get the milk out and put it on trays. I practiced in my mirror at home and then stared into Victor's eyes the way I saw actresses in old melodramas do on *NBC Saturday Night at the Movies*. With so much to be learned on television programs and films shown past my bedtime, there was no need to go to school, except to see Victor.

Victor took his job seriously, making sure all his cartons were lined up evenly. Finally, toward the middle of the school year, he spoke to me.

"Do you want that?" He pointed to a half-eaten cookie on Sharon Slater's tray.

Shocked into silence, I shook my head no and handed it to him. The conversations continued.

> VICTOR: "Do you think we should put the milk on the left of the tray and the cookies and napkins on the right?"
>
> ME: "Whatever you think is best."
>
> ME (trying to sound interested): "Do you think we should split the room vertically or horizontally when we pass out the trays?"
>
> VICTOR (as if I were a moron for asking): "Vertically, of course."

These exchanges over the garbage bin were the highlights of my day.

Although I insisted I was way too old to have a babysitter, we had one, named Irene. She was fifteen, and I liked to think of her as my friend who was coming for a visit. Her boyfriend, Tom, was sixteen, had curly long blond hair, and was cute in a disheveled sort of way. Irene looked like a model in *Seventeen* magazine; she was tall and thin with deep black eyes and the longest eyelashes I'd ever seen, ultrastraight black hair that she didn't need to blow-dry. One evening, I noticed a ring on her finger with a small oval stone that sort of changed color when she moved and the light caught it in a different way. She said it was a moonstone. Tom's grandfather passed it down to him, and he gave it to Irene to signify that they were going steady. I had learned about going steady while watching *Bye Bye Birdie*. In the movie, Hugo (Bobby Rydell) gives Kim (Ann-Margret) his school pin.

"That's how we did it in my day," Nana Ida told me. "We called it getting pinned." The idea of a boy giving you a piece of jewelry to signify he loved you was definitely romantic.

"I want to go steady with Victor."

"Beth, boys are more interested in sports and playing with their friends at this age," my mom advised. Irene and my grandmother agreed with her, all of them sitting around the dining room table. "Maybe you should think about becoming a Brownie instead of spending your time daydreaming about Victor?"

One day after school I flopped dramatically on my bed. "But I love him."

My mom stroked my hair and rubbed my back. "Victor is six. He isn't ready for a relationship. I don't think he even brushes his teeth every day."

By the middle of the year, Irene broke up with Tom to move to California. I realized, with the help of my grandmother's urging me to hang out with the girls during recess, that I was cleaning up cookie crumbs and half-finished milk cartons, chewed-up straws and crumpled candy wrappers from kids' pockets just to be close to Victor. "You might want to be a bit more nonchalant next time," Nana Ida advised. "Maybe you don't have to volunteer to clean up garbage to be close to a boy."

She and my mom began to laugh, and I began to cry. They came in for a tight three-way hug. "By the summer, I promise, you will love another boy," my mom said. I didn't think she was right. My heart belonged to Victor and it wasn't changing any time soon.

By fifth grade, although I still pined for Victor, I had a short-lived romance with Brian Murphy. Our relationship consisted of his throwing me off my bicycle and pulling out my seat when I went to sit down in the library. When he pushed me down and broke my front tooth, my mom told me she thought Brian had anger issues and spoke to his mother, who said he'd been in therapy since he killed their goldfish. By then it was too late. I invited Brian over. He took my turtle, Taffy, out of her tank and ran around the house with her, eventually knocking into a chair, squishing Taffy in the process. Brian and his mother came over the next day.

"Brian, go talk to Beth," his mom insisted.

"I am very sorry I killed your turtle," he said, with a grin only I could see.

He presented me with my first gift of jewelry, a sterling turtle charm. "Not to replace Taffy but in remembrance of her," said Brian's mom.

"Okay, can we leave now?" Brian asked. I put the charm in a drawer, where it remained, and where later in my life other consolation gifts of jewelry would go that were given to smooth over arguments and hurt feelings or to apologize for situations that couldn't be patched up with diamonds or gold.

My tooth was fixed. I got two new turtles, and Victor was still in my heart. Although he mostly played sports and still didn't seem interested in any one girl, I was completely and utterly miserable.

While lying on the hammock and writing in my diary, I could hear Nana say to Mom, "She used to love to sing the songs from *The Sound of Music.* Now she is obsessed with the Beatles' 'Yesterday.' She is ten and singing, 'All my troubles seemed so far away.' She should believe in 'today' and get involved in some sort of activities to keep her busy."

I had a flair for the dramatic and a penchant for unrequited love that would follow me into my adult life.

Finally, toward the end of the school year, Victor, whose hair had grown shaggier, started going out with girls. Unfortunately, the first one wasn't me.

It was a new girl named Gail who had strawberry blond hair and big green eyes. She would shimmy between Victor and Steve Schultz with her tray at lunchtime, asking, only after sitting down, if the seat (that really didn't exist till she squeezed into it) was taken. Despite all my mom's advice, there was something she wasn't teaching me, something she was missing, and therefore something I'd never know. What did guys like? What did they want? Victor and Steve were the two best baseball players in our class; I wondered what it was about Gail that got their attention.

Then one day, Gail inexplicably moved to the opposite end of the lunchroom, with no warning, obvious argument or reason. I was beginning to think there was no rationale when it came to boys, love, what makes someone like you and what makes it right or wrong.

Just as I was figuring this all out, Victor stopped by my lunch table. "Hey, Beth. You know there is a dance next Friday night, right?"

"Yep." I was trying to look at ease and wondering whether he could see my heart pounding through my tie-dyed top. I tried to hide the perplexed look that said, *You haven't spoken to me since first grade. I wasn't sure you remembered me, and now you are about to ask me to the most important event in grade school?*

Of course I didn't say these things. I didn't say much. I said, "Dance."

"Well," Victor said, digging his hands in his faded jeans and shuffling his feet, "I thought you might want to go with me."

"Sure." I was monosyllabic yet again. Eventually more words started forming in my brain and we set a time; I gave my address, and we concluded that his parents would take us and mine would pick us up.

Once I had the power of speech back, I said, "I thought you and Gail were together?"

"No, she dumped me after baseball practice for Steve. I think she was just going out with me to get him to notice her and it worked, and then he dumped her for Jen."

Lucky for me, I thought.

Nana Ida disagreed. "You should play hard to get. You don't want to be anyone's rebound relationship."

"I want to go to the dance with Victor. I have been waiting forever. Can we worry about the details later?" This would be another problem that would follow me well into adulthood: waiting, sticking around too long and worrying about the warning signs after I was most definitely warned.

Victor and I did the twist, slow danced and, although I attempted to lead, we generally had fun that evening. I wore a minidress with a new pair of dangling turquoise and sterling silver earrings.

He brought me a Coke and chips, shook his hair out of his eyes and took off his ring from his right hand. "Would you want to wear this? I'm not sure where it will fit." It wasn't a goofy school ring like those some of the other guys had given to girls in my gym class. Instead, it was a silver band inlaid with turquoise that he had gotten on a trip to New Mexico. Victor was cool. "It matches your earrings." He touched the bottom of one gently.

"Does this mean we are going steady?" I asked, filled with wonder and joy and love.

"Yep," he said, and then slipped the ring on my thumb, the only finger it fit.

"This was worth waiting for all these years." I didn't mean to say it out loud. Victor smiled and hugged me tightly. The next day in school, Victor held my hand at recess and carried my books, and we did all the going steady things I'd seen other couples do. He would pull me behind a teacher's car and kiss me hard, mouths tightly closed. These were the best days of my young life. We ate Linden's chocolate chip cookies at lunch, which he bought at the school cafeteria. We split our sandwiches and talked about the other "couples" that got together at the dance.

I noticed others who were going steady and what they wore to seal their bond. One of my friends was wearing a sun pendant that her boyfriend borrowed from his mom. Another wore a puzzle ring.

Not only did I have Victor; I was, in spite of my new braces and my hair, which had begun to frizz that year without warning, one of the cool kids.

After a few weeks, I saw that the ring was turning my thumb a shade of dirty lime green, but there was no way I was taking it off, except at night to sleep and only then because I curled up with my face on my hand and it dug into my eye.

"Can we try just cleaning it with some silver polish and

lots of soap and water?" my mom asked when she saw my finger.

"Oh God, no!" What if we ruined the ring that meant I was with Victor? It was tarnished and worn and could have used an ultrasonic cleaning. Now I know that certain types of silver and how much alloy is used will turn my skin a sickly shade of green and eventually cause little itchy bumps to form.

The rash was spreading and the green was getting deeper in hue when Victor came up to me during lunch one day and said, "You're a good kid. You're funny; you make me laugh a lot, but I don't think I really want to go steady anymore." Almost as quickly as he made the decision to give me his ring, he took it back. It was spring and he did it outside at recess where everyone could see. Two days later, his ring was on Sue Thomas's finger.

It was a while later that Sue tapped me on the shoulder and asked, "Did Victor's ring turn your thumb a strange color?" I held up my finger, which was now a faded, almost scarier color of bluish green. She thanked me and started wearing his ring on a chain around her neck.

"You will find a new guy, I promise you," Nana Ida said.

"Someone whose ring won't give you gangrene," my mom chimed in.

"I love Victor, and I don't think I will ever understand what happened."

It took a while, but eventually my thumb went back to its original state.

CHAPTER 3

Engagement Watch

T HE FIRST ENGAGEMENT ring I ever saw (that wasn't worn by a friend's mother) was a surprise that fell out of a Cracker Jack box when I was six. It was more of a faux pink sapphire than an exquisite D flawless diamond. My taste grew more sophisticated that year, and I began to covet the larger, gleaming colorless solitaires in gumball machines. I'd place the nickel in the slot and turn slowly, wishing that the little plastic bubble would deliver my glimmering gem rather than a slinky snake that would pop out once you twisted the top off the casing. "It might be easier and less expensive to go to Woolworth's and buy one," my mom would say when I'd make her go back and get more change. There was something exhilarating about winning the prize instead of purchasing it (although I do think we spent around a hundred dollars in nickels before it actually fell out of the slot and landed in my hand). Eventually I went on to buy the five-and-dime versions, which gave more choices in cut, shape, size and metal color. Yet none of these imitations could ever evoke for me the personal story of my parents' marriage.

My dad had presented my mom with a watch instead of a ring for their engagement, and she accepted it.

In my thirties, after a number of relationships—men whom I let get away and those who started out promising and ended up promising themselves to other women and/or men—I thought more about that watch while trying to piece together the reasons why I could not close the deal; why I remained a freelancer instead of being offered a full-time position. Or why, as my grandmother questioned, I "couldn't just find the one . . . or someone already." I wondered if the engagement watch had predetermined my romantic fate from childhood.

By age six, rather than playacting marriage scenarios, I learned how to tell time. I knew that dinner was when the big hand was on the twelve and the little hand was on the seven. I knew that if my dad wasn't home by then, he would call, either to tell my mom that he was working late in the city and would be staying over or that he was delayed an extra day on a business trip. I knew my mother was worried. I knew she cried herself to sleep on those nights.

In my mid-teens, when I began dating, I became obsessed with guys being late, convinced after ten minutes that they were not showing up. Waiting for the phone to ring caused even greater anxiety, so much so that I thought Dorothy Parker's "The Phone Call" belonged in the self-help section. If a guy would forget to call at the designated moment, I just knew he had lost interest. If fifteen minutes had passed, it was quite clear he was breaking up with me. None of this actually happened, but it's a neurosis I still battle today.

But back then, all I could fathom was that we were different from everyone else I knew. It would have been a much more interesting story if my parents had been children of the sixties and eschewed all things conventional. No luck. They met in the late fifties. They were both raised as lower-middle-class reformed Jewish kids in Brooklyn. My maternal and paternal grandparents were first-generation Americans of Russian descent; their tradition was to signify their love for each other with beautiful but simple gold wedding bands. My father, Mel, was the middle child of Annie and Willie, and he had an older sister, Glory, and a younger brother, Shelley.

My mom, Shirley, an only child, had a huge extended family of cousins, a nurturing home and a seemingly functional childhood, until you looked a bit deeper. Her dad, Papa Rubin, was a real worrier and didn't trust "just any guy" with his daughter, so he had one of his brothers, Sam, an NYPD detective in Manhattan, come to Brooklyn to follow her whenever she went on a date.

"It was mortifying to have a 'report' on every guy I went

out with," my mom confessed, "but worse, Uncle Sam was six foot four and extremely hard to miss. He'd be watching me from his car or from the other side of the street, where he'd sometimes blow me a kiss or mime me a hug."

Although my mom loved her family, she dreamt of having her own place, dates without her uncle's shadow and a career as a stage actress. To support her dream, she worked as a runway model so she could afford to take classes at Stella Adler and move to the city.

My father worked for a textile company before opening his own mills that produced menswear fabrics. I'd ask him to tell me the story of how he met my mom; he'd repeat it as many times as I wanted to hear it. "I walked into a coffee shop in the garment district—the type of restaurant with no-wait service but where you waited in line with tray in hand—ordered my usual, a pastrami on rye with mustard and pickles and slaw between the bread, spotted the most incredible-looking woman I'd ever seen, eating a fruit salad. She was a mix of Audrey Hepburn and Elizabeth Taylor, five foot six, a perfect body, the smallest waist and longest legs I'd seen, dark hair, large almond eyes and heart-shaped lips. I walked right up to her and said, 'I am going to marry you.' And then I tried as nonchalantly as possible to walk away and find a table."

While I always loved this chance meeting, my friends wanted more.

"Is that it?" they would ask, those who had parental stories of fairy-tale proposals: rings in champagne glasses, poetry in fortune cookies and trips to far-off lands. As far as I knew, this was all I had to work with.

"I kept telling him to leave me alone," my mom always chimed in when my father got to the part about declaring his intentions. Handsome, with sea blue eyes, he began to frequent the same restaurant to see her and to charm her with his quick wit and compliments, enough for my mother to start dating him. I heard stories of their going out to dinner and dancing at famous NYC restaurants and clubs.

I never heard of the actual proposal, or whether there was an actual proposal. They went together for about a year and then planned a wedding.

There was no ring and no enchanting engagement story (and, according to my mom's uncle, no rap sheet on my father, "just a gnawing sensation in [my grandfather's] gut"), but there was a beautiful wedding with a custom-made dress from one of the high-end bridal collections my mom worked for as a fit model. It was made of a French embroidered lace fitted bodice, a straight-off-the-shoulder cap sleeve neckline, a skirt of organdy tulle that grazed my mother's ankles and a veil of the same fabric with a little floral wreath around her head. There was a classically cut tuxedo that my father wore that made him look elegant and dashing, like a 1950s movie star. They got married in a temple and stepped on the glass for a long happy future. My mother wore my paternal grandmother's garland-style choker, and they exchanged two thin gold wedding bands.

BETH BERNSTEIN

When I was nine, I asked for a more detailed explanation about the watch. "It was much more practical than a ring and more affordable too, and I really needed one. We didn't have a lot of money starting out." I felt that something basic and true was missing, but I never pushed my mom into talking more about it. Later, we all found out it was an authentic art deco timepiece with an enamel dial, small diamond accents and black onyx—a fine antique. "Who knew?" said my dad, who got it for a good price from a friend of a friend in the jewelry business, who also had no idea what it was worth.

Even after my dad's business took off, he still never got my mother a proper engagement ring. She never mentioned it. She wore her watch proudly, and it attracted much attention and many compliments—from strangers on the street, other mothers she met while dropping me off at school, on vacations and at the dry cleaner's, basically wherever she went. It became her signature. Yet sometimes I wondered how she felt when they went out to dinner with friends, when all her peers were upgrading to better stones, trading gold for platinum settings or receiving entirely new rings for important anniversaries. My father gave her gifts of South Sea pearls and a Van Cleef & Arpels pin, offered to smooth over arguments and to mark her thirtieth birthday. There were the business trips, when they would stop in London and Paris and my father would buy my mom clothes from the trendsetting designers of the time, Biba and Courrèges. Then they went to Italy, where he had his fabric mills and where he purchased her fine leather goods. Eventually my father would make these trips alone.

I'd overhear Nana Ida and Papa Rubin talking when my father's late nights and business trips started to become more frequent.

"He's a playboy. He has never had any family values." Papa Rubin would pace up and down. "A real ladies' man. He's going to make her miserable. We should have stopped it." Papa Rubin was the most loving man but could be direct when he felt strongly about anyone hurting his family, especially his only child and daughter.

"We couldn't have. She was determined to marry him. And we should be thankful for the three grandchildren we now have. We will help her figure it out. She will be fine," Nana Ida said. There was some Yiddish thrown in for dramatic effect in the retelling of the story. The biggest shock came when I learned that Nana Annie confided to Ida, "I told her she was marrying the wrong son. She should have married Shelley instead—much more compassionate, loving and trustworthy."

In the earlier years, I remember all of us being happy. We went from a cabana at Long Beach to the bungalow in Monticello, where my father, like all the dads, would drive up on weekends and we'd stay on throughout the summer. When he'd get there, I'd get all excited. I would love to watch him and my mom go swimming together and get dressed up for the nights going into town with friends. It was the 1960s, and my mom and her friends wore shift dresses, long disco ball earrings and chin-length angular Sassoon haircuts. My dad always looked impeccable as well; he was in his late twenties, his hair turning prematurely salt-and-pepper, distinguishing him and highlighting his blue eyes.

They looked like the perfect couple, surrounded by grace, taste and style. My father loved to sing and belted out Tony Bennett and Bobby Darin songs on long car rides. "C'mon, Beth. You know the words; sing with me." Soon he'd have my brothers, mother and me humming off-key but laughing in harmony. But the arguments grew louder inside the bungalow. My mom questioned strange phone numbers on matchbook covers and why my dad had to skip coming to see us three weekends in a row.

"You are being ridiculous," he'd say in the most condescending tone he could muster. "That's the dry cleaner's number," he would snap. "Stop being absurd." Maddened by his patronizing, she'd call and find out what she didn't want to know.

After that particular summer, we left our apartment in Queens for a six-bedroom, four-bathroom house on two acres in the suburbs of New City, New York. We kept moving toward a more superficially comfortable place, where the grass was greener and the air fresher and our surroundings were safe, where my father could go through the motions of being a husband and a family man. When my mother was decorating and unpacking, my grandparents came over to help.

"Are you sure you want to do this?" they asked my mom. "We can take you and the kids in until you can figure out everything."

"He needs patience. He needs security. He needs someone to stand by him," she replied.

"He needs to think of you and his kids. You are building a life here and he is traveling around to God knows where with God knows who," Papa Rubin said.

"Business, to visit his textile mills to make sure they are running smoothly," my mom said.

Late at night, I could hear them arguing. I could hear my mom on the phone with my grandmother, explaining that the more trips my father took, the more he'd leave his gold band at home. My mother would take the watch off and not put it back on for days at a time. They still played tennis and went to dances at the country club. But the facade was fading and they were growing farther apart. Eventually, the watch stopped and my mother did not fix it, tucking it away deeply into a drawer. Later in my life, I realized that my father's ambivalence was always present, not only in the absence of a ring, but also in his incapacity to be faithful.

Unlike a diamond ring—the stone symbolizing longevity and the band meaning continuity and eternity—the watch came to represent my father's inability to form a lasting bond. I've realized that, for much of my life, I carried on this tradition as well. Recently, I had my mother's engagement watch fixed. I wear it every now and then. I've always kept my parents' wedding picture on my nightstand for my own sense of continuity and to keep them close to me. Whenever someone sees it, they compliment me on what a beautiful couple they seemed and how, like two figurines on a wedding cake, they looked like they belonged together.

CHAPTER 4

Love Beads

I T WAS 1972, the summer of my parents' divorce. Wayne Newton had a hit single, "Daddy Don't You Walk So Fast," about leaving his daughter, and I played it over and over again, hoping it would help me make sense out of my own life.

I was twelve, and in our small community of New City, New York, where families like mine moved from the boroughs for better lives, safer schools and a bigger homes, everyone was still happily married, except for us. While my friends' parents were discussing wood paneling and whether or not to screen their porches, my mother and father sat in the den, discussing alimony and child support. They agreed it would be too traumatic for me to leave before I finished junior high school. My father decided that my mom, brothers and I could spend one more year in the house before my memories would be wrapped up in newspapers and packed into boxes and our home, which was once freshly painted with rooms to decorate, would be turned into the great divide of which parent would get what.

My grandmother tried comforting me. "You're young, you'll still spend time with your dad on weekends, and when you move, you'll make new friends. You have your whole life ahead of you." But I didn't feel young anymore. I had just learned how to French kiss, got my first hickey, and I became a "woman" earlier that year, getting "my friend," which I had considered a very odd expression since I could never go swimming with it and it always made me feel bad. My adolescence had turned quickly into young adulthood as I learned about the more sophisticated language of my father's affairs and the woman he was leaving us for.

My mother, liberated from my father's adultery and the years she tried to stay together and fix their relationship for the sake of my brothers and me, began seeing a therapist, went to EST and reread *I'm OK, You're OK*. When Erica Jong's *Fear of Flying* came out after the yearlong separation in 1973, she thought that it was a form of self-help.

Her path toward self-discovery created more confusion at a time when life for me was already about learning how to adapt and readjust. Although my father was the one who moved out, my mother was acting out—rivaling a teenager trying to gain independence by cutting ties, staying out all night, dating and rebelling against her family. I began to feel as if I had lost not only one parent but both. In my mother's process of "finding herself," she had traded in her short, perfectly layered Sassoon haircut that framed her face for a Jane Fonda wash-and-wear *Klute*-style shag. She started taking adult education classes in the evenings instead of helping me with my homework, relying on me to heat up Swanson TV dinners to feed my brothers, as a substitute for the big home-made meals she prepared when my dad was still living with us. She talked about needing her space and about us all having to go through a period of adjustment, but she wasn't helping us through it. Instead, she spent most of the time with George, her French Canadian artist boyfriend she had met in a painting class and who was seven years younger than she was. And yes, if I have to admit it, he was gorgeous—six foot two with deep green eyes and a head of curly light brown hair. He dressed in baggy, worn Smith's painter's pants with T-shirts with sayings on them and high-top sneakers, and he was about as mature as Eric, my nine-year-old brother.

The summer of my parents' divorce, the mother who once propped me up on her vanity while with adoration and pride I watched her get ready for a night out as she clasped on her choker-length Jackie O–style pearls and zipped up her chic little shift dress, had taken to wearing *my* jewelry and clothes.

She wasn't just dressing *like* me. She was in the kitchen, singing along with Helen Reddy, "I am woman, hear me roar" with my love beads around her neck and my bell-bottom Landlubber jeans emphasizing her long legs. In between lyrics, she was ripping open Hostess Twinkies and powdered donuts with her teeth. "Breakfast?" she asked. I shook my head no.

All I could do was point out the obvious. "You are wearing my stuff!" And upon closer inspection: "Is that my peace sign too?"

The truth was she looked better in my outfit than I did. She was thirty-five and although we wore the same size, my mother's body was more proportioned, with her tiny cinched waist, her flat stomach and her swanlike neck. Mine was more awkward. Earlier that year, when I had worried about my poufed-out stomach and love handles, she affectionately assuaged my concerns, explaining they were hormonal changes that would straighten themselves out "any day." But she had been saying it for months and nothing seemed to be shifting, flattening or evening out. I looked at the way *my* jeans highlighted her small hips, with her stomach almost indented, and how the multistrand beads cascaded gracefully over her halter top. I yelled at her with a mix of envy, confusion and rage, "You look ridiculous."

"Hey. Watch how you speak to me. I'm your mother."

"Why aren't you acting like it?" I missed the woman whose closets I used to raid, while she helped me shimmy her Pucci print dresses over my head, while I clopped around in her platform shoes, her bangles clanging up one arm, her charm bracelet dangling from my other wrist, as I tried to imitate her, my idol and the woman I had loved and admired for as long as I remembered.

"I had no time to go shopping for new clothes—I am seeing George tonight and needed something more fun to wear."

She had forgotten that she'd promised to take me for a new swimsuit for one of the biggest pool parties of the summer and instead told me I needed to take care of my brothers. I had grown out of the tops of the prior year's bikinis and didn't know what to do. Taking care of my younger brothers was something, at age twelve, I had not looked forward to, nor was I particularly comfortable with it, because my mother worried about everything. She left notes taped everywhere—to the fridge, on the kitchen counter, by the alarm system, on the front and side doors and porch, all concerning what to do in case of any kind of emergency she could imagine. This left me with the sinking feeling that I was completely responsible should something happen to one of my brothers in my care. I was already making sure they weren't jumping from staircases or falling into lakes, talking to David's camp counselors when he was upset or trying to get Eric, then nine, to stop smoking Pall Malls. There was only so much I could handle at my age.

Despite my state of general adolescent confusion and rebelling against her changes, I couldn't forget the mother who loved and nurtured and listened throughout all the years before: helping me through my shy phase, sleeping in my hospital room all night when I had my tonsils out at age five, teaching me how to wrap my hair at night to straighten it for the morning. She talked me through every breakup between puberty and adolescence, of which there were many, since at that age, relationships lasted about as long as a game of Seven Minutes in Heaven, with the exception of my five-year obsession with Victor and my three-year on-and-off relationship (more off than on) with Jeremy Glick, from sixth through eighth grade.

"I'm supposed to be the one dating and she is supposed to be home taking care of the boys." I had called my grandmother for advice.

"She's trying to figure things out. George is a passing phase, but he makes her feel good about herself after all that she went through with your dad. She still loves you very much. Give her some time. She's also looking for a place to move and a job in the city," my grandmother said.

For months after my parents had separated and my father moved out, I could hear my mother crying in the middle of the night, big, heaving, long sessions of grieving that I wanted to make go away. She went from smoking one pack of Benson & Hedges a day to two, and burned breakfasts most mornings as she talked endlessly, wrapping the long phone cord around her nervously while speaking with her two closest friends. She told them blow-by-blow details of my father's cheating, how she found out and about his moving in with the woman he left us for (this woman would become my first stepmother). My mother finally gave up on cooking and fed us an array of sugary cellophane-wrapped confections. She'd go to the supermarket to buy milk, forget what she'd gone for and come home, where I would hand her the list she had left on the dining room table. There would be nights I would get out of my bed, lie down next to her and play with her hair, rub her back and tell her that it would be all right, that my dad didn't know what he was doing, that he'd realize what he lost and he would be back. In the mornings, she started asking me to get my brothers ready for school and told me I needed to take care of them and keep them safe. I knew I had to get my father back into the house for all of our sakes.

There were boy/girl parties, rounds of spin the bottle to be played, diaries to fill up and summer camp, which a whole group of us were signed up for. The last thing I thought I needed was to be different from my friends. Fearing I might be dropped from my group, I told no one that my father had moved out or anything about the impending divorce. I didn't even tell Jessica, my best friend since the fifth grade. Although I trusted her to write in my diary and with all my secrets about guys, I could not figure out the words to explain about my parents. Jess and I looked so similar, people mistook us for sisters; we both had blue eyes, long dark hair and braces, and we were both thrilled when Susan Dey, our idol, flashed her braces on *The Partridge Family* on national TV.

I ran away to her house often and said it was because I had an argument with my mom or was sick of my brothers. I ran away, mostly for effect, hoping my mother would continue to call my dad the way she did the first time she didn't find me at home. After that, whenever I'd arrive at Jess's, her mother, Eileen, would call to tell mine I was safe. When Jess and I had met in the fifth grade, our mothers realized they had gone together to Erasmus High School in Brooklyn, where Barbra Streisand, Neil Diamond and some other famous people went. Our mothers' common background brought Jess and me even closer together.

I was too much of a coward to go any farther than her house, and so I'd make a big deal of packing a bag and leaving a note that said unless my parents tried to work it out, I was not coming back. Then I wrote one that was less angry and tried to express how I truly felt:

> *Dear Mom:*
>
> *We both are very anxious right now and have to make an effort to try and hear each other out. Things are happening in both of our lives that aren't so great. You might think the problems at my age are really stupid, but they are really big for a thirteen-year-old. Believe me. Maybe you would like to discuss them instead of going*

out with George one night. PS Do not discuss or show this letter to him. And then I can try to help you with your concerns as well. Parents would be surprised how much kids know. We both are guilty now of not trying to have the relationship we once had, so let's try. Oh, and there is nothing I want more than you and Dad to get back together again. Do you think you can try and forgive him? I don't have to tell you that you both still love each other. But let's discuss it in the morning when we both have time to sleep on it.

It stayed on the counter unread, and I left for Jess's.

Mostly it was a good escape, listening to our favorite Grass Roots and Tommy James songs on the jukebox in her basement. We exchanged macramé friendship bracelets and wrote poetry and song lyrics together, and we tried to create cleavage by bending over into our bikini tops and tying them really tight. Eileen was the most beautiful woman I had ever seen, besides my mother, who wasn't an actress or a famous model. She had deep turquoise blue eyes and Carly Simon–layered hair, and she taught Jess and me how to use a little liner under our lower lids. Both of Jess's parents seemed cool: They listened to Carole King and James Taylor and took us to Greenwich Village. We went to a poetry reading, ate strange food in dimly lit restaurants and bought incense and dangly earrings on the street. It was the first time I saw same-sex couples embraced in passionate kisses, old and young people hanging out together and such a rich tapestry of cultures nestled into a small but vastly diverse space. For a girl sheltered in the suburbs, used to the freshly manicured green of the country club, the Village symbolized freedom. To a thirteen-year-old whose mother and father were going through a divorce, it also represented that people could be different and still belong, something I desperately needed to feel—and did on that night. I told Eileen I wanted to live there one day. Twenty years later, I moved into an apartment about four blocks from where we ate and have been living here since.

Since running away wasn't a viable option for trying to get my parents back together, I tried to figure out other ways and began to imitate the illnesses I saw on *Medical Center*, the ones with names I could pronounce, and symptoms I could figure out how to fake, hoping that if I was sick, I could get my parents worried enough to be in the same room together and talking about something other than the "check not being on time." I might have seen some version of this on TV, where I learned so much about the ways of the world.

So, one night when I got what the nurses in Nyack Hospital's emergency room (a few towns over) would eventually call the worst case of food poisoning they had ever seen— from a Big Mac, no less—my mother refused to believe me. It took several hours of writhing in pain, and vomiting, before she called my dad to come watch my brothers so she could take me finally to get help. By the time we got home, my father was fast asleep on the couch. My mother covered him in a blanket and brought me upstairs to my room, apologizing for waiting so long and telling me the story about "crying wolf"; then she proceeded to ply me with liquids and Jell-O until I could eat again. It was the first time since my father had rushed me to an emergency room when I went into anaphylactic shock from a bee sting when I was seven that he also was completely freaked out. He called the woman he was living with to say that it was a real scare, I was still dehydrated even after the IV and he was staying the weekend to make sure I was okay. From then on, my parents would continue to spend Saturday nights through Sundays together, my father lying to another woman besides my mom, saying it was making it easier on his kids this way.

I thought I had won him back, that this couldn't mean anything else but that my parents were getting back together. I overheard my mother say to my grandmother, "I finally am the other woman, and it's a hell of a lot more fun." When I think back on it now, she was putting up a front to let him back into her life, and neither of them was ready to let the other go completely, especially when my mother had started dating again. My father could not accept that there could be another man except for him.

"You're confusing the kids, and you need to make a clean break for all of your sakes. This is no way to live," my grandmother told her. My mother shrugged it off. She had been seeing the therapist and "started to feel like [her] own person again." She started talking like one of those self-help books she had read.

My father finally did ask her to get back together. I was all excited that I'd have my family back, that there would once again be big breakfasts, my parents and brothers sitting around the huge pine table with discussions of the Watergate break-in, and that my father would stop acting like "Tricky Dick," lying to us as Nixon seemed to be lying to the country. I dreamt we'd again have the rich, happy, lazy chatter that filled up Sunday mornings: Did my dad feel like mowing the lawn? Were sectional sofas too spare and modern? Did going out for Chinese taste better than bringing it home? But my mother turned him down.

My brothers and I were required by my mother to join in on the therapy sessions once a month with her analyst, Marcia, who wore ultralong earrings and flowing caftans and sat cross-legged on the floor. She asked my mother how she felt about not taking my father back. "Empowered," my mother said.

Marcia asked me how I felt; I said, "Duped." I didn't answer when she asked what I meant until I was alone with my mom and brothers in the car. "You wanted to hurt Dad, but you wound up hurting all of us with this game of yours." I felt horrible about what my father had done and I was happy my mother was no longer crying herself to sleep. But I continued to tell her off. "You shouldn't have let us believe that you were going to be with him, that we would be a family again, that we might not have to leave our friends. You should have been honest and fair." By the time we were home, she was sobbing, bent over the steering wheel, her head in her hands. And although I meant what I said, I couldn't stand seeing her like this and apologized for pushing her so hard.

In the weeks to follow, I found Mitch, my new boyfriend, kissing one of my friends on the side of where the changing rooms were at the pool party. I couldn't wait to get home and talk to my mother, but George was there. I left and went back to Jess's house, where "on-again, off-again Jeremy" was walking home to his house across the street from Jess's. He said, "You are all wet."

Jess was still at the party, and her parents were out. He told me to come inside with him and dry off. I found comfort in the fact that we had known each other so long and so well that I trusted him once again. (Another pattern I would repeat with men into my adulthood.) He gave me a few towels and a big T-shirt and we started playing pool, only to find myself ten minutes later in a tug-of-war with him for my bikini top. He called me a prude and told me to grow up, and I ran out. I wandered around, trying to figure out all the things that had happened. I wasn't sure why Mitch would be kissing someone else—was I not good at it, not as pretty or funny as the other girl? I questioned what had caused him to stop liking me from one day to the next and if he ever really did. I realized that this must be similar to how my mother felt when she found out about my father's affairs.

Soon after my dad stopped staying over on weekends, my mother's fashion choices grew more like mine—peasant shirts, large rings, choker necklaces, elephant bell-bottoms and clogs. We had traded roles. I felt I was now the adult, as she had asked me to be, when all I wanted to do was figure out boys, do well in school, continue to be popular, have straight hair and a flat stomach and live in the house where I had grown up. But she was reliving her teenage years at the time in my life when I needed a mother the most.

One night when she was out with George, I was taking care of my brothers and I heard noises downstairs. I called the next-door neighbors, whose phone number was on my bulletin board one of the many numbers my mother left in case of an emergency. As frightened as I was, my knees starting to buckle, I tiptoed gently upstairs and got my two brothers into one room, telling them that we were playing a game and that the winner of the prize was the one who could be quietest. The neighbors told me to call the police, who arrived quickly. I heard my mother open the door and start speaking to them. As I walked down the stairs, I noticed she was wearing tennis shoes, which she never did in the evenings, and I realized I had called the cops on her by accident.

"Is this your mother?" one of the policemen asked. I was speechless, staring at my love beads that she continued to wear.

"Answer them," my mother said. My brothers came running out to see what all the commotion was and jumped into her arms, which was enough for the cops to shake their heads at me and tell me, "There are real crimes we need to be on call for."

"Why didn't you say anything?" my mother asked when they left.

"I have no idea who you are anymore." I started to cry uncontrollably.

Instead of punishing me, she grabbed me and held me tightly for a very long time, sitting on the bottom stairs with my two brothers wrapped around us.

At the end of that August, my mother broke up with George, admitting he was a bit immature. I had a new boyfriend, a nice guy who was a great kisser and the first person I told that my parents were getting a divorce. He told me his were too and that it would all be okay. I knew he was lying, but I was glad I could get the words out. In years to come, all my friends' parents, including Jess's, would split up.

I told my mom about my new guy, and she said she was glad I was over Jeremy. "He looked like a monkey." She made me laugh again after a very long summer.

After Labor Day, my mother and I went on an outing to the mall to buy back-to-school clothes for me and what I was hoping would be more grown-up fashion for her new job at a large clothing company in Manhattan (where, a few years later, she was promoted to VP and then senior VP).

We tried on mood rings to see what color they would

turn and puka shells, which had become a big trend after David Cassidy wore them on *The Partridge Family*. She asked if they were right for her; I shook my head no. And then with my allowance, I snuck away and bought love beads for her so she wouldn't have to borrow mine anymore.

CHAPTER 5

The Single Solitaire

T HE ENGAGEMENT RING was a three-carat solitaire, sparkly, glistening, light bouncing off from
every angle. It was bigger, more brilliant and had
more shine than any diamond I had ever seen; at twenty-
one, I hadn't been in contact with a gem that came close to
the essence of this one.

I was used to receiving my initials or tiny flowers and
hearts set with diamond chips, which, if you blinked quickly
you would probably miss. This was the type of gift I received
from guys, friends or family, for my sweet sixteen, Valentine's Day, graduation and birthdays.

Looking down at the fiery stone made me squint as if
looking directly into the sun. I was amazed at its size, my
mind racing and the dizzying fifty-eight facets of the brilliant cut whirling around in my head. The magnitude of this

rock spoke to my life in that moment and to how my future might unfold.

I studied it, brief glances at first, trying hard to take it in, to keep breathing, to stop fidgeting. I didn't notice the tears trickling down my face; I could not feel them. I was completely in awe, in the moment, and I seemed to be hovering outside my body, unattached to my limbs and monitoring my movements and reactions as if watching myself in a film.

I never thought it could happen in this way, not under these circumstances, not with a ring like this and not with the guy I had loved for six years, from the time I was fifteen years old.

No. It didn't seem real, possible or imaginable that Cello would place this gleaming round cut diamond, set in platinum, on someone else's left hand.

They say that diamonds can cut glass, but no one tells you that they can also splinter your heart. No one told me that years later pieces would still be there to remind me that my first love, the guy with whom I had my first song and lost my virginity, would propose to . . . someone else . . . a girl I went to high school with, who I never thought would have any effect on my life with the exception of helping me obtain a pass to get out of gym class.

Her name was Linda Granita, and Cello began to date her during one of our off-times. Thinking back on it now, the ring was the type that today might show up on rap stars or *The Real Housewives of New Jersey.*

The bling-y, high four-prong setting and in-your-face styling was definitely being thrown in mine, so there would be no question Cello was no longer with me. I ran into Linda everywhere. She was in the supermarket, left hand grabbing a head of lettuce, and then again in the pizzeria pointing at a pepperoni and cheese while I paid the cashier. At the Saks at Riverside Square Mall across from me in the shoe department, she was pulling on boots with the twinkle of her ring bouncing off the foot mirror and back at me. I even caught a glimpse of the huge rock while she was signing her name at the DMV. I'd run into Linda more times after Cello and she had gotten engaged than in the four years of high school we attended together.

I could have written it off to fate, but the truth was that I was warned early on that Cello and I were not destined for an enduring relationship.

I met Daniel Costelli (nicknamed Cello) when I was fifteen. After two months of going out, he invited me to dinner at his house. I was nervous and full of giddy excitement that this meant I was truly part of his life, that his parents wanted to meet me, my heart doing aerobatic acts like the first time I had seen him. I wore a light lilac angora sweater dress, my hair just trimmed with wisps to frame my face and fall over my shoulders, blown out perfectly straight for the occasion. I wore simple makeup as always, a touch of mascara and a hint of lip gloss, and an Elsa Peretti heart from Tiffany & Co. that my mother had bought for me. After the introductions, over cheese manicotti and Italian sausages, we talked about Cello's science project and how his parents had met and emigrated from their hometown of Naples, Italy. Without any segue or warning, his father looked at Cello sternly and said, "She's a Jewish girl from a broken home. You can't marry her. We won't allow it." It took Cello a few moments to register what had just been said before mouthing, *I'm sorry* to me; while I was twisting my napkin in my lap, his father, in a mix of broken English and Italian, continued. "You have fun with her now, and then you get serious!" I wanted to run out the door. I wanted Cello to stick up for me, but he said something in Italian, which I didn't understand, and then quickly changed the conversation.

Although I had never felt as much for another guy, we still had two years to go before we made it to senior prom and I had not yet even thought about my dress; this was as far into the future as I could manage at the time. Marriage was the farthest thing from my mind.

We had only fooled around fully clothed and had long make-out sessions in between figuring out what our favorite Fleetwood Mac album was and talking about Peter Frampton's next concert. We were two young kids discovering each other, but none of it was a foundation to build a life, home and kids.

But Cello was an only child. He told me that his parents talked constantly about wanting the most for him, which meant a marriage that would give him the things they thought they couldn't provide, none of which included Hanukah gifts or the question "Why is this night different from any other?" from a girl whose parents couldn't stay together.

I had not encountered anti-Semitism before and felt bruised, dejected and confused. The parents of Manny, my mother's boyfriend (who became my stepfather three years later), were also from Naples. Lorraine, my stepmother, was a mix of Portuguese and Italian heritage. Manny and Lorraine were from Catholic backgrounds, but neither of them was particularly religious, and we celebrated all holidays in both homes. In mine, Christmas was always my favorite. My mother decorated a huge tree and had an open house for all of Manny's six siblings and their kids, my brothers and my friends, many of whom would joke that our house was like the UN, with every nationality, ethnicity and age group represented by all the people we knew and loved.

Fort Lee, where we had moved from New City two years earlier, was a melting pot of cultures. Originally, I was concerned that, as one of the first divorced kids in New City, I wouldn't fit in to my new surroundings and would have to fake it as I had earlier.

While there were still many stable families in the town that held the entrance to the George Washington Bridge—easy access as an escape route to Manhattan—I soon realized that many of the other kids' fathers were not living at home either.

Fort Lee was a town almost stereotypically characterized

by divorcées, men who wanted to date them, "connected" dads, many of whom were behind bars, and Irish American fathers who still might have resided at home but who lived most of their nights in different types of bars, ones that served free pints during happy hour and had last calls on the house before closing time.

In Fort Lee, every Sunday seemed like Father's Day, and we all visited our dads, no matter where they were. I began to feel right at home.

When I told my mom and Manny about what had happened during dinner at Cello's, Manny was enraged. "I'm going to have a talk with those people. No one speaks to you like that." He stomped around the living room floor, finding imaginary lint, a habit when he got angry or nervous. I begged him not to go. My mother, thinking I was young and that the relationship would eventually run its course, calmed Manny down and told me not to go back but to have Cello come to our home.

We broke up many times over the years, partly because of his parents, partly because I was going away to Boston University and he was staying in New Jersey to attend Rutgers. We dated other people but continued to come back together. During one of our breakups while I was away at school, he began to see Linda, her family being from Palermo and in construction. His parents decided she was the girl for him. Her parents decided he would fit into the family business and that they would get engaged after he graduated. They bought him the three-carat ring to give to her. His life had been planned way before we ever met, and he would settle into it long after I would be gone. It took Cello ten months after her parents purchased the ring to finally propose. The almost-flawless-quality diamond would be much more than just a glimmer of a memory but part of a story that would replay over and over again in my head of the boy I first met and couldn't let go and all the moments I tried to recapture of the younger version of us, long after *we* were gone and I should have moved on.

Back then, I couldn't have known exactly why I would not let go, except that in the beginning when he was around, the rest of the world, life, school grades, college applications and anything else I worried about, seemed to disappear.

I'd first started going out with Cello in tenth grade, two months before the night when his parents sealed our fate. I lost my heart to him almost immediately, lost my fear of heights *only for him* on a summer day hanging out on the Cliffs, along the Palisades that overlook the expanse of the New York skyline and the steep rocky and scary drop to the Hudson River, where Cello held my hand tightly and helped me inch out slowly to the edge, from where I still clung to a tree. We lost our virginity to each other, when I was in eleventh grade and he in twelfth, late one humid afternoon in his twin-size bed.

I eventually lost him, after I went to Boston, when I was concocting excuses to come home and see him on weekends, turning away guys in college who were smart and handsome and whom my dorm-mates referred to as good "husband material." I was more concerned with being with Cello than with what this meant, but in the years to come, I'd realize it had more to do with putting a ring on my finger, not on someone else's.

When Cello and I first met, I literally fell for him. He lived one town over and went to a different high school, but we had friends in common. I'd been hanging out at the baseball field in Fort Lee where a group of us went every day after school. I was wearing a peasant top, long mesh-style earrings with tiny beads, thin bangles, and white jeans. I scrunched down, knees bent rather than sitting in the grass so I would not get green stains on my ass. My legs locked and my entire bottom half sort of froze in that position. A mutual friend said, "Beth, this is Daniel Costelli—we call him Cello for short." He reached his hand out saying, "Nice to meet you." As I tried to get up, I landed hard on my butt in the muddiest part of the grass. He helped lift me and we both laughed heartily, making me feel at once instantly at ease and also queasy, my stomach bottoming out as if I were on a roller coaster rather than on a suburban stretch of lawn.

He was one year older, funny, slightly shy and sweet. He was the most beautiful boy I had ever seen. He also had no idea that every girl wanted him. This was probably what I liked about him most (and that he chose me out of all who gathered around him as if he had just figured out the questions and answers to the college boards). He had black eyes with long thick eyelashes and wavy hair, the whitest, straightest teeth, an olive complexion, perfectly shaped lips and one dimple on his right cheek when he smiled. He was five foot eleven, to my five foot five. We shared a love for Philly cheesesteaks, the Beatles' *Abbey Road* album, "Octopus's Garden" in particular, had a similar sense of humor, and we cracked each other up constantly. We became fast friends. He had his license and would pick me up in his parents' beat-up Buick, and we'd go to the movies and drive around listening to eight-track tapes of Rod Stewart, the Eagles and America. He could remember almost every *Honeymooners* episode, and I was a captive audience when he would imitate his favorite scenes. We'd hang out in friends' basements playing pool or at the Dairy Queen where he worked part time, and I'd meet him for a cigarette and beer in the back of the shop.

From the time we met, it took Cello about six months to finally kiss me. I had almost given up on our ever being more than "friends" when Cello found out I was becoming slightly interested in another guy named AJ (whom I would date later on and who would become my closest friend for the next thirty-five years). Cello asked me if I wanted a driving lesson. We were outside the apartment building where I lived in the visitor's parking lot. While I was scooting over him to change from the passenger to the driver's seat, he took a deep breath, his hands cold and clammy on my back, helping me move, and his heart beating quickly. Just when I was settling in, he pulled me closer and awkwardly kissed me, the steering wheel stabbing me in the ribs, but all I could feel were his soft full lips against mine, his tongue gliding gently and then probing a bit more. I had never felt such a raw desire, as if every part of my body wanted to be touched and held by him, such that all I could see was him, drawing me in closer like the lyrics of some Bruce Springsteen song (intimate and full of youthful passion that feels like it's burning down to your toes and back up your spine). We continued to kiss for two more hours. When he dropped me off in front of my house, he said, "Well, it's about time that you kissed me." The dimple appeared, and I thought I never wanted to be in anyone's arms but his. It was three a.m. when he drove off, and I woke my mother, with a cup of Maxwell House instant coffee. Once she shook the sleep off, she listened intently, her large almond-shaped eyes widening, her smile getting bigger as if the news were as exciting and important to her as to me. Or maybe she was just tired of hearing me say every day, "Why doesn't Cello like me as more than a friend?"

We waited until the morning to call my grandmother. I had no secrets when it came to the maternal side of my family. Once, when I was older, I got into the zone of a little too much information. My mother had said, "Good to know, but maybe you could go easy on the explicit details." In my mother's and grandmother's eyes, I may have been a tad manipulative and dramatic, perhaps a lot dramatic, but I was beautiful, smart, fun, brilliant at whatever I set my mind to do. My love life might have been simpler if I could have found some male who felt the same way about me as my mother and grandmother had.

Cello's and my time together was spent going down the New Jersey shore to Long Beach Island and sleeping on the beach or in his car, wrapped in a large blanket and each other. We went to concerts in Manhattan and then Philadelphia, when I lied to my mother and Manny that we were going to Great Adventure so they wouldn't worry about us being in "massive crowds with too many people drinking liquor and doing drugs." It was perhaps the only time I didn't tell my mom the truth, when I wanted to go somewhere with Cello and not have her worry.

Late at night we'd snuggle up in my house when my mother and Manny were out for the evening, with him reading my poetry about . . . him and me analyzing *The Canterbury Tales* for his English assignment. After the first kiss, the rest grew more passionate. The first time we had sex was in his bed, when his parents weren't home (the only time I would go to his house after meeting them that one evening two years earlier), and I turned over the saints protecting him. It was tender and quick, and he borrowed a condom from his father's drawer. It was the first time for both of us, and we moved instinctually and tentatively. "I think it will get better for you," he said, and all I wanted to do was stay curled up in his arms, playing with the few stray hairs sprouting up on his chest. I came home and told my mother and asked her if I seemed changed, different, and she said, "Oh God, now you're going to be obsessed with him."

"Now?" I asked.

Over the years, sex got better and better. We learned together, how to move with each other, and it was all natural and full of soulful kisses and lingering playfulness that was erotic in its innocence and the growing knowledge of our bodies. While at BU, during our breakups, I'd try to be with other guys, but it never felt right, never felt the way it did with him; I'd come home from college in between holidays and breaks or just for the weekend.

Even after he started seeing Linda, I continued to be with him; neither one of us was able to give each other up completely. I justified it by saying he was with me first. We had grown up together, hurt each other, playacted adult dramas and we always came back.

Once the ring went on Linda's finger, he changed drastically. He started sleeping with every woman he could get into bed. Many of those times he left with them in front of me; other times he left with me, on nights I saw him in bars and in dance clubs. I held on tightly to my fonder memories and other times I felt nothing but anger for him. Yet, I still wouldn't give him up.

The closer the wedding date got, the more women he wanted to be with and the more I felt left out and left behind.

I finally screamed at him, "You are a puppet. Your parents have always made all your decisions for you and now they have even chosen whom you will be with. It won't last, and you will wind up alone, an old man with nothing." It was mean and angry, but I couldn't, didn't, want to take it back. He grabbed me and said, "I don't love you anymore. I love her." I'd lived my life around seeing him; I'd let go of guys in college who might have wanted a future with me, always running back home to him.

When I described the ring to my mother, every detail committed to memory—the platinum shank, the marquis-shaped side stones, the tapered band—on the wedding day, she held me in her arms and said, "He's an idiot and doesn't deserve you."

"Cello is the only one I will ever love, and I will never be able to imagine myself being with anyone else." While I didn't remember I had said that about my grade school love, Victor, or my sixth grade through junior high school crush, Jeremy, my grandmother and mother did. But they listened and tried to soothe me, with big gooey hugs and even gooier chocolate-covered caramel marshmallows that we ate straight out of the box while my mother asked me to use tissues if I was going to slobber all over her Ralph Lauren paisley couch.

I had not gotten out of my pajamas or bed for three days prior to or on the wedding day, wrapped in my sadness the way I wore my terry bathroom robe belted tightly around me. My grandmother was up from Florida, where she and my grandfather had retired ten years before. She and my mother took turns with offerings of Häagen-Dazs chocolate chocolate chip ice cream, Mallomars, and against my grandmother's usual aversion for cellophane-packaged cakes, they offered up a smorgasbord of my favorite Drake's confections. While unwrapping a Yodel, my mother said, "Honey, I think maybe you need to brush your hair—we don't want to have to cut the knots out of it." My grandmother got in on the action, pointing a Devil Dog at me and suggesting, "Maybe a little shower. I will go in and run the water for you."

"But it's raining." I moved into another position on my bed.

"So do you want us to take the soap outside?" my mother asked.

"Wait!" My grandmother stopped biting down into the cream filling. "This is good. Rain on a wedding means the marriage won't last." My mother nodded her head in agreement, still trying to coax me into the shower.

I had figured out the time it would take for the reception to begin, and, just at that moment, the sun started coming out, brightening my room and blindsiding my moment of temporary calm.

"Ah," my grandmother noted quickly, "it's clearing. She will see through him and want to leave. The marriage will be over before you know it."

"And by that time, you will have moved on and found the guy who was meant just for you," my mother added.

I never knew where they got this stuff, if they made it up

as they went along, but the fact that my grandmother was eating Yankee Doodles, my mother was offering more zany explanations and they were able to curl up next to me when I smelled worse than a pile of my brother's dirty laundry was enough to snap me out of the moment and to know I was loved. These women might not be able to teach me how to land a man, but it was consoling to know they would always stand by my side.

Years later, to help me with a different breakup, my mother tried a new tack. It was just around the time I was turning thirty and really starting to freak out about winding up alone that she came up with the ingenious idea. "You should have no problem understanding men. You have two younger brothers you can learn from." This was her aha moment?

"They are two sports fanatics who live and breathe football. They are lazy and would be happy if their life revolved around eating pizza and Chinese, and never having to dress in anything but their team jerseys. They have no idea about girls; they both come to me for advice."

"Exactly," my mother said. "You are getting the point."

It wasn't until after they were both married and I was still single that I understood the gist.

When I wasn't meeting anyone I was interested in dating, my brother Eric said, "It's because you only like pretty boys. You have to go for the bald, fat ones."

After a breakup of a relationship that went on longer than

it should have, I asked David, who was then married with two kids, why it didn't work out. "Maybe you ask too many questions. You are sometimes like a lawyer trying to get at the truth. Men don't like that."

About another guy, David had an epiphany. "Hey, maybe he figured out that your fear of heights includes the balcony in a movie theater."

It went on like this a couple more times till I stopped asking. They were men; they were giving me reasons (albeit sometimes in jest, sometimes because there were no answers, and other times because they really didn't know what to say). But those answers I didn't want or need. I wanted it sugar-coated with milk or dark chocolate and cream filling like my mother and grandmother had given to me.

Then one day my brothers were going through a box of photos and came to me with pictures of me from the height of my relationship with Cello. "Look at how beautiful you were, and you didn't know it. You saw yourself only through how you imagined Cello saw you," David said. He was right. I was by no means model pretty, but I was in fact quite cute, with big deep blue eyes and long dark hair, tall with a small delicate frame outsized by perky breasts.

"The point," Eric continued where David left off, "is that you are now spending too much time with another guy, questioning what you are doing wrong. You are an incredible woman, and we don't want you to waste any more time looking back on this. Please face it and move on."

My mother had been right. Having brothers might not have given me the emotional goo that kept me stuck together, such as she and my grandmother had provided, but they too would take over in their own male way and give me confidence when I needed it.

Sometimes, I think the reason I held on to Cello was twofold. I truly loved him and was so afraid to feel the loss of saying good-bye to someone who knew me so well and with whom I'd experienced everything for the first time. But I also think I was trying to keep it going because if I let it go after so much time, what would all those years have meant? I'd be left with nothing. Never realizing until years later, after I'd held on again to a different relationship, that the more I was not letting go, the more I wasted on something that was no longer good or right or healthy. But back then, all I wanted was the way we first were, much like I had wanted my parents as I had idealized them to be.

A month after the wedding, I saw Linda's wedding ring. It was not an all-around diamond eternity band but a half circle of diamonds in the front. Their marriage lasted for six months before they were separated and Cello was calling me again. I met him for drinks one night to hear what he had to say. His father, whom I hadn't seen in years, came to find him and bring him home. He didn't acknowledge me; he just threw some money on the table, took Cello out and left.

Cello and Linda got back together after four months. He continued to cheat with women I did not know and did not want to know about anymore. He kept calling. I never answered. I'd had enough and could not go on with it any longer. No epiphany; no grand-scale happening. I'd finally grown up and out of him, the younger us, the pain, trying to fix something that was never meant to be.

I could finally let go of the vision of us that I had held on to, always trying to mold us back into that couple who first kissed in the car. I thought if I gave up, there would be no meaning in it, realizing much later on in life that this was self-fulfilling: The more I held on, the more time I would spend and the more time would be lost.

He was hurt when I would not see him anymore.

At the ten-year high school reunion, I ran into Linda in the ladies' room, the ring twinkling brightly under the fluorescent lights. While she put on lipstick next to me in the mirror, I noticed an anniversary band on the other hand. Her wallet was bursting out of her handbag with photos of her two kids.

Five years later, he called me to tell me he was getting a divorce, that her parents had caught him with another woman and that he was scared he was going to lose his kids. He asked if he could come over to talk. I said yes. I had known him since I was fifteen. After he explained the story, he said, "I will never forget what you told me about being a puppet; you were so smart so young." Had I been, I would have walked away when I said it, but I was glad he acknowledged after so many years that I had been right.

At the twenty-year high school reunion, neither of them was there, but I saw Linda a few days later, her fingers bare, with a band of white around where the brilliant solitaire had once been. I had no band, only the memories that would linger of a first love that should have ended long before it did and the hope that one day I would find the single ring for me.

CHAPTER 6

Claddagh Ring

"Y ou're not who I thought you would be," Liam said, bending down to grab my duffel bag at Dublin Airport. *Excuse me?* Feeling deflated, I half smiled at him, then threw my knapsack over the shoulder of my Schott motorcycle jacket and adjusted my tights under my short black pleated skirt. "But I'm glad you're you," he continued, his voice cracking as he pointed to the elevator. He had a beautiful mouth, which turned into a big, lopsided, mischievous grin when he smiled. The one time I had seen him, when he lived in New York, his sandy blond hair had been pulled back in a loose ponytail that stopped at the nape of his neck. It was now cropped shorter, held in place with gel except for one piece that kept falling into his bluish green eyes, and it showed off his straight nose and high cheekbones. He was twenty-eight, three years younger than I, but he looked more boyish than the time we were introduced at a friend's birthday party. After I traveled three thousand some-odd miles, he had absolutely no recollection of meeting me.

"We need to go down the lift." I followed slightly behind him, guessing he was around six foot one. His brown leather bomber jacket and gray cashmere sweater hinted at his broad shoulders. He was undeniably cute, much more so than I remembered. "Great to have someone over from New York. This place is bleeding boring, it is. Oh Christ. I mean if you've grown up here."

"You really have a way with words," I said, looking him square in the eyes and trying to keep a poker face.

"Bollocks, sorry. Let's start over." He dug his hands into his worn, baggy Levi's and shuffled his Doc Martens–clad feet. "Really happy to have the honor of showing you around our fair city. Please let me know what places you want to see."

"Great opening. Maybe you should have led with that?" I lifted the straps of my duffel bag, which were sliding off him, back up onto his shoulder, meeting his eyes and breaking into laughter. He let out a sigh and smiled the lopsided grin, apologizing for being an "eejit."

I was glad he seemed nervous; he wasn't smooth like some of the other Irish guys I'd met back in New York, one in particular, Sean, Liam's childhood friend, who'd come home with me at four a.m. after a party. There was no sex, only sleeping and cuddling together, not that he didn't try. I awoke to his making toast and jam, singing me Gaelic love songs and spinning yarns about his youth growing with up Liam and some of the other "lads." He made it sound as magical as the Lucky Charms commercial with some adventure and sex thrown in, all of which had initially ignited my fascination with Ireland.

When I'd first met Sean, my boyfriend of the past two years, Jay, had broken up with me on my birthday, after asking me to hang in and see him through the bad times and his bouts with depression. When I was going through a rough time of my own with my job and needed help moving from Chelsea to the Village, he promptly started dating someone else while still seeing me. He asked me to wait while he figured things out; when I mentioned how much he had hurt me, he was thoughtful enough to recommend that I see a therapist and then had his psychoanalyst find me one to help me "get over him." I called Celia, my English friend, who advised, "Leave the analysis to him and get out of the house and have some fun." I was warmly welcomed into her crowd of Irish and English transplants, who hung out in East Village pubs, drinking lager and Guinness, telling stories, having parties and good times while looking out for one another. They immediately took me in and made me feel like one of them, teaching me slang. Many of the Irish and English guys tried at one time or another to "have it off" with me, which I took as a compliment. I was desperately in need of male attention and to feel sexy again. But mostly I felt safe in the camaraderie of knowing where to find one another, that someone was always there to help me hail a cab or walk me home late at night. I developed short-lived crushes on the guys and a longer-term love for the cultural nuances. There was something in particular about Dublin, the language and the lilt—the poetry of Yeats and the soulfulness of the street that Alan Parker made bigger than life in his film *The Commitments*, which had just come out at the end of summer 1991. In retrospect, I was looking to be anyone but myself or to be with anyone who wouldn't bring me down the way Jay had done. I wanted to be in the moment, forget the past two years and how foolish I had been, staying so long in a relationship yet again, and to create new memories.

I had a hankering to go visit some old friends in London, then go on to Dublin, a place I would find to be beautiful, with its greenery and stone bridges over running streams, but that had no running hot water except if you woke up at the crack of dawn. It was a place where life was simple: Everything you liked was *deadly* and everything you didn't, *poxy* or *shite*, and where Jay would have been considered a total *wanker*.

Celia had called Liam to see if he would show me around. He had been living in Manhattan but had gone back to Ireland for six months to help out his mother, who was described as a "bit batty." His father had passed away when

Liam was young, and his married sister, who had four kids, called Liam for some help.

With the assistance of a Michelin guidebook, I picked a family-owned bed-and-breakfast close to Liam's home.

And then I went for a crash course in behavioral modification techniques. In my attempt to flee Jay, and myself, and to feel something different, I forgot one looming detail—I was terrified to fly.

I hadn't been on a plane to Europe in eight years. I had three weeks to overcome it. Peter Shubert, Psy.D., said it usually took six weeks, but he thought he could speed up the process since I'd already paid for my plane tickets.

I'd been battling this fear since I was twelve, when I flew out to LA with my younger brothers to visit my father, who moved there for a year. We had an emergency landing with oxygen masks and heads curled over knees and everything else I've never ignored again in the safety demonstration. I had gotten over it enough to be able to fly with friends or relatives and colleagues for my job.

I was a freelance fashion editor/stylist for women's magazines and newspapers. The last time I'd gone to see the runway shows in London and Paris with Celia, I spent eight hours in nonstop turbulence coming home and it landed me right back where I started, hyperventilating whenever I thought about taking off.

My mother sent mixed messages. "Go see the world," she'd freely advise, and then for short trips to my grandmother's in Florida, she split her children, husband and herself up on different planes, like the royal family, "so if one of the planes didn't make it, some of us would survive and be there for each other." I think she always felt guilty for sending us alone on the LA flight. This time she was perfectly clear in her message.

"Are you kidding me? Why the hell are you going three thousand miles away to a country you don't know? I could see if you were American Irish, tracking down your ancestors. But you are third-generation Russian, and it may just be colder in Ireland. You like to know that your primary doctor is on call. You like to phone me at eleven p.m. on the dot each night. And, most important, you don't know this guy!"

I calmed her down to get her on board with the trip, although, unfortunately, not on the plane with me, which I still had to deal with.

The behavioral therapist took me out to JFK airport, where I was to be leaving from. He sat me down by the gate and asked me to imagine everything about the flight from checking in to landing. "What about crashing?" I asked. "Or trying to open the doors and leap out in midair?"

"Yes, definitely imagine that too," he urged. I cried. I screamed out and had one intense anxiety attack, all while sitting in the terminal drinking a Coca-Cola. "You did great. You have one hell of an imagination and you're going to be fine." He was truly pleased with the outcome. I was going to ask for a refund but was too busy breathing into a paper bag. "If you take yourself through the trip again for three nights before you leave, you will work out all your fears." I thought it was "bollocks," but I did what he said because that was how much I wanted to get away. I packed way too much and took off on my journey. He was right; I'd gone through the worst of my fear and calmed down an hour into the flight, realizing there was nothing I could do anymore. I could freak out or choose some films on the back of the Virgin Atlantic seat. I chose three movies, chain-smoked and put a good-luck coin my grandfather Rubin gave me on a chain around my neck, which would be the start of a talisman necklace that would grow more symbolic with time. Magically I landed at Heathrow. Upon seeing the Aer Lingus gate, I realized I'd have to take another plane in two days and decided maybe I could take the ferry from London to Dublin. If I did, it would be twelve hours and freezing compared to forty-five minutes and climate controlled, so I braved another plane.

I had known Liam was a bit confused about who I was before I left. I met him while he sat on a bar stool in New York, Guinness in hand. Celia introduced both her friend Rena and me at the same time. We both had dark hair and light eyes, but we had very different body types. Later, Liam would tell me he felt too politically incorrect to ask Celia whether I was "the thin or fat one," and he imagined I was the latter. This explained why he was happy when I wasn't who he'd "been expecting," and I was pleasantly surprised at how compelling his initial awkwardness was.

He suggested we have a beer at the pub before going to drop my bags off at the B and B and deciding where we should go for dinner.

When I explained how I'd been searched after deplaning, he told me I'd been felt up by security. "Did you think that men are allowed to pat you down in Ireland when everywhere else in the world there are woman guards?" I was jet-lagged and anxious about meeting him, and I had heard that security was very strict about the IRA and planes coming from Heathrow into Dublin.

"Yes, that part is all true, but they copped a feel," he teased. I was mortified by my naïveté, but something about my embarrassment was making Liam settle in and feel more relaxed.

I told him stories about his friends back at home and my stay in London, with the exception of two parts. There was a pool going on, which was high stakes by this time. The odds were *not* on whether I would "shag" him but on how long it would take. Between the first and third night? What hour? Morning or evening? The pool had gone transatlantic. Even the guys I was staying with in London placed bets. One of them said, "You are definitely going to do it, so it's best not to have odds against yourself." Clive and Owen, a gay couple who lived in the same house, agreed. Clive said, "The guy is way too adorable to pass up and not many women have." (*Oh, great endorsement,* I thought.) I hadn't felt any attraction to him during our brief encounter in New York and thought they were all nuts or living vicariously.

The second story I didn't reveal was that I had originally packed most of my wardrobe. "Oh, we have to consolidate you." Owen shook his head. They made two piles, a smaller one "to take" and a huge one to leave at their house. Lace camisoles and mesh tops for layering under cardigans, short skirts, leggings and my high Doc Martens boots all were traveling with me. "Hey, I'm a fashion editor," I said. Clive was too and came back with what sounded like a copywriter's blurb: "You are not going for cozy and warm. You are a sensual, tough yet tender New Yorker."

"Your skirt and your shiny tights are deadly," Liam said as he handed me my Coca-Cola. I told him I drank only wine every now and then since nothing else really agreed with me. "Not really conducive to Dublin, but tomorrow night we can go to a French-style bistro that recently opened," he suggested. I thought about the pool, looked at my watch and wondered whether anyone had taken odds on "an hour after she gets off the plane." He leaned in and started kissing me in the pub, which continued in the car on the way to the B and B and in the restaurant, which turned into a dance club after eleven p.m. We kissed in between dancing to every song from the 1970s through the 1990s, including doing the "Time Warp" (again). And we wound up shagging at two a.m. Dublin time that first night.

Not only had I gotten on a plane, but I was snogging in

public, which I just found out meant kissing, and I was diametrically opposed to public displays of affection, especially in bars, movie theaters and on any form of transportation, all the places we'd make out for the next three days. In the meantime, I was lying to the nice churchgoing Catholic couple who owned the B and B about Liam being my fiancé, not seeing him for four months and that our betrothal was planned for when he was due back in New York. It worked, and he was allowed to stay in my room, which was where, we were told, "all the priests came and stayed when they were passing through Dublin."

"I'm Jewish, and I'm going to hell," I whispered to Liam. He unpeeled my layers of cashmere, lace leggings and black Wonderbra and panties, then pulled my hair to the side and me on top of him and said, "I love your knobby knees."

"Is that how you got all those women to sleep with you back in New York?"

He smiled in that mischievous way, kissed me and said, "You're beautiful, and you've got gorgeous long legs, but— see?—they are knobby like mine." And so I tapped his knee gently with mine and then curled up in his arms. He said, "I drank more than usual tonight; I'm a bit concerned about brewer's droop." This was another expression I'd never heard but could figure out.

"Say *film* while kissing me," I asked.

"You're a bit wonky but okay. Fil-um." His tongue rolled

the word out in my mouth. I loved the way the Irish musically put an extra *u* in the word.

We both started cracking up, which I'd hoped for to get his mind off worrying, and we wound up staying in bed until two p.m. the next day, much to my B and B owners' chagrin.

"So, this is Dublin?" I said. "I had heard the natives were friendly." I cuddled in closer to him. Two p.m. turned into three p.m.

"I'm a bit knackered," he said.

"Translation please?"

"Tired generally but after sex, tired in a really good way." It would be one of my favorite slang words from then on.

He had to do errands for an hour, check on his mom, shower and change. The moment he left, I was panic-stricken when it dawned on me I had just slept with a guy on the first night, within hours of meeting him for the second time (after literally talking to him for ten minutes the first time we were introduced), in a foreign country where I knew no one, had no doctor or dental referrals and had run out of cigarettes. What if he never came back?

He was fifteen minutes late, which seemed like fifteen days in the seemingly endless loop of these thoughts.

During the next few days, we went to Trinity College to a Beckett festival; saw *The Commitments*, he for the first time and I for the second, since he said it was finally playing in Ireland; saw the poorer sections, beautiful greenery and the inside of many pubs where soccer was on TV and where the idea was to stay warm, hang with friends and keep Guinness in business. While fiddling with my earrings, one side a dangling lock and the other a key, he asked if they represented the way into my heart. "My very own Irish poet," I said. He charmed me and romanced everything he spoke about. I also liked that he knew about jewelry and took me into a shop in the center of town. It had modern and antique styles and was where he told me he preferred pieces that had symbolism. He pointed to a Celtic infinity knot charm, explaining, "It represents endless and continuous love. The Claddagh ring is the Irish engagement ring, which has two hands holding a crowned heart. But it can be worn with different meanings, depending on which finger and how you place the heart, facing in or out." I'd seen them on Bleecker and Eighth Street in the Village.

"Those are really bad Mexican-made silver copies. Not authentic. For you it would need to be genuine," he said, and got excited when he spotted an 18K gold version with a deep emerald heart. The shopkeeper told us that an American tourist couple had asked for it to be custom made but then changed their mind to a sapphire instead. "And so we have this beauty here for you fine young couple." Liam said we'd take the infinity knot charm, which was raised and recessed to emphasize the interlocking circles and swirls of the design. He hooked it on the chain with my grandfather's coin. "A souvenir for you to remember your stay and so that our friendship endures," he said. I was confused by the word *friendship*, feeling like I just had a passionate three-day affair, the memory of which would forever stay in my mind. Maybe this was how he was ending it? But then he kissed me again outside the shop and in the next pub stop to see the soccer scores. I was making up for all my misspent teenage years of pushing guys away in public venues, and I was snogging and copping feels everywhere, in the land of chippers and confession.

Before leaving, I gave him a silver ring, which I'd worn on my thumb since college, and he put it on his pinky. I said for "eternal memories," and he tickled me.

"I can't imagine not seeing you for six more months, until I get back," Liam said as I got onto the plane. I forgot for the first time in my life that I was on a plane and instead remembered all the experiences vividly.

"She got shagged," Owen said, immediately giving me the once-over when he and Clive picked me up at Heathrow.

"How could you possibly know that?"

"You are beaming," said Owen.

"C'mon—let's go out and celebrate, and you can tell us the whole sordid tale," they said, teasing me, and took me to yet another pub back in London.

Liam called the house the next day to say good-bye before I left for the airport and a week later after I got home. "I'm coming back to New York early, in time for your birthday. I want to see what we are about. I will be there in two weeks." A poem arrived airmail in between phone calls.

"But you weren't supposed to be back until February. It's only October," I said, shocked, flattered, confused, not quite sure how I felt about this.

"Don't you think we should figure out what happened?" he asked tentatively.

"Yes, I want to see you. I just want to make sure that you are aware of what you are doing. We can talk and stay in touch for a few months, getting to know each other more." I wanted to feel the same way I'd felt in Ireland, but I also didn't want Liam to regret a decision he had made in haste. I couldn't believe I was thinking so clearly. Who had I become? Just a few weeks before, I had impulsively taken a crash course in fear management to fly three thousand miles to get away from myself and had sex within hours of landing with someone I barely knew. Rational thinking was not one of my strong points when it came to men. But I think the experience had finally gotten me over Jay and also proved I didn't have to be trapped by my fears.

"I'll be there on the second of November, three days before your birthday."

My mother kept calling: "You have nothing in common. It's just a reaction to Jay."

Liam arrived on November 2 as planned and told me he needed to go talk to his ex so she wouldn't hear from someone else that he was back and seeing me. They had been together since they came over from Ireland to the States four years before, and he had broken up with her a couple of months before he went back to Dublin, before we met. "She didn't take it well," Liam said. "I'm sad I hurt her like this. She was my best friend and looked out for me." I asked him if he needed more time. But we wound up spending every night together for the next week. He gave me a photo of us for my birthday in a beautiful antique silver frame. We'd fall asleep listening to Aretha Franklin every night. I wasn't sure if I wanted my family to meet him yet but asked if he wanted to come for Thanksgiving. A group of our friends had a tradition of getting together every year, and he asked me if I minded if he went with them. "Not if you help with what I have to prepare," I urged. Liam could peel potatoes quicker than anyone I'd ever met, and before I'd even washed my hands, he was zipping off the skins and boiling a huge pot of water. My favorite comfort food was and still is mashed potatoes, and he made them exactly the way I liked them, with small lumps that melted with the smoother texture in my mouth. Later, as we were falling off to sleep, he said, "I wish I could be with you every night."

"You can't move in with someone just because he makes the best mashed potatoes you ever tasted." My mother was trying to get her point across with humor, which didn't always work when I knew she was right but when hope and passion took over insight and instincts.

"The potatoes are really good; maybe she should keep him around at least through Christmas," my grandmother teased during Thanksgiving dinner.

And then she got serious. "We love how you can open your heart, but try to do it a little more slowly. Don't give all of yourself before you really know this guy." I loved my family's honesty, their ability to say what they felt and their quaint habit of never minding their own business. If they did, I wouldn't have known who they were.

Between Thanksgiving and Christmas, I'd half taken my family's advice and given him only two drawers. He parked his bicycle in my small apartment entranceway, and I had to slide my body sideways past the seat to get in and out of my house. As the holiday approached, he started drinking more, eating and sleeping less. Nights were spent in the East Village with the guys and harder liquor. "Take me to bed," he would say, slurring, the playful Irish lilt wilting into a blur of half-intelligible words. He cuddled with his arms around me, apologizing and saying he hadn't drunk like this in a very long time and it must not be agreeing with him. We shopped for his family and mine.

We went to see the Black 47s at Paddy Reilly's Bar. Liam had grown up with one of the guys in the band, and when they covered his favorite Bob Marley song, "Three Little Birds," they asked him up on stage. He sang to me, so cute, alive, charming and just a wee bit drunk, which was becoming his normal state.

We decided to get a Christmas tree together, and I was ecstatic. Sometimes I felt as if I was riding his highs and lows. It was the first year my mother, stepfather and brothers were all going down to Florida instead of having Christmas at my mother's home, with the huge tree, the incredible ornaments and lights, the open house with massive amounts of food, all of which my mother prepared. She knew why I turned down going with them and understood, lending me my favorite ornaments that she had collected. Liam bought me a few more, and we got mistletoe, glittery tinsel and an intricate crystal star I picked out for the top.

We decided to invite all our mutual friends for Christmas Day. We went to a food emporium in the West Village, which sold English and Irish delicacies. Liam explained that maybe the word wasn't *delicacies* but more like *familiarities*— sausage rolls and kidney and mince pies. I filled in with my own recipes for some traditional American food and ingredients for a sugar rush of desserts.

On Christmas Eve day, he was like a kid with a secret he couldn't wait to tell. While we were in pre-preparation mode, getting ready for a late-night party, he handed me a small heart-shaped box with a tiny bow. Upon opening it, I was overwhelmed; it was the Claddagh ring we had seen in Dublin. He had sent his sister back to the store, hoping it would still be there. "It's so beautiful." I kept looking at it inside the little velvet-lined box and hugging him.

"Can I put it on your finger? I want you to wear it tonight and tomorrow when everyone is here and every day after that." He took my right ring finger, placing the ring on with the heart facing down. "Your heart belongs to me and mine to you." He pointed to the ring I'd given him in Dublin Airport that he never took off. I'd never been so happy on Christmas Eve. It was the first time he'd ever seen *It's a Wonderful Life*, and he cried with me through the last part like my mother and grandmother had done when I had watched it with them every year before. I wore a red velvet dress with a hint of Lycra to the party, and he danced with me for most of the night and showed my ring to all our friends. I wasn't prepared for how drunk he got or how his friends had to help us get him into a taxi.

"Let him sleep it off; he'll be fine in the morning," they said. I showered, dressed and began to get ready for our fourteen guests, preparing the rest of the food and table settings, the desserts and the drinks, then running out to find more ice. I tried to wake him, but he kept asking for another hour. When he finally got up, he called his mother, cried and told me we had to cancel and he was getting back into bed. I'd never seen him depressed or unable to function before.

"Please try and get it together." I held him. "We can't cancel; it's too late. They will be here in an hour. I will help you through it. They are your friends. You've known them longer. Plus we have mince pie." I wasn't getting through.

"I can't face anyone, and there is nowhere else to go. You are my home now." The tears streamed down my face as I sat through the doorbell and phone ringing and didn't move. I was going against every part of my being for him and I couldn't stop. Gifts were left with my doorman with notes to call; people were worried that one of us had wound up in the hospital. The next day, he explained it away, and everyone accepted the story except for Sean, who hugged me tightly and said he understood. I didn't. But during the rest of the week and through New Year's, Liam was on his best behavior and back to being playful and passionate, telling me he loved me, holding up my hand with the ring and saying I held his heart in my hands.

By February, I figured out he had a problem with alcoholism. I felt foolish that I hadn't picked up on how bad it was; but most of the guys I went out with got sloshed from time to time and, like Liam, none started drinking until after work. I think that was what threw me, that and the hopefulness that he brought to me in the beginning. It spiraled over the next few months when he had too much and he'd get sad and more needy of my attention, scared that I would leave him, yet disappearing all night with pints of Guinness and shots of scotch. But then he'd stop for three weeks to a month, and all would return to normal—whatever that meant now. I didn't know, except that during those times we would turn into the two people in Dublin who didn't want to let each other go. It was the first time in my life I didn't share something with my mother. I knew what she would say; I knew what I needed to do but didn't want it to end. I longed for the continuity and connectedness of the circles in my knot, but they had been broken. Unlike the

Claddagh ring, which held a heart in its hands, I didn't trust mine in his. By May, he'd gotten back together with his ex. Sean explained, "He loves you, but he's scared he will never live up to your expectations. She's like a mother to him; unfortunately for him, for you and for her, that's what he needs."

I ran into her a few weeks later. I'd only met her once when I first started hanging out with that crowd. She asked if she could talk to me. "He needs me, and he could have never been with you long term. He loves you, but it will pass." I wished her well and walked away. This time I had gotten a unique ring but still had not found the right guy for me.

CHAPTER 7

Pearls of Wisdom

"THIS IS THE best dressed funeral I've ever been to," my friend Jodi whispered. With the exception of AJ, Jodi was my closest friend in Fort Lee. She practically grew up in my house, drove with my mother into the city and asked her advice when she first started working in the fashion industry, where my mother was a senior VP of a sportswear company. Jodi had known me for eighteen years and knew what would make me laugh.

"Definitely," I said. "My mom would have been impressed. It's a packed house and resembles a Donna Karan runway show." As Jodi and I tried to crack more jokes, AJ worried about when I was going to crack.

"It's not normal that you haven't cried yet," he said. "You were so close."

I thought if I started, I would never stop, never get out of bed, never be able watch an AT&T commercial again without breaking down.

"Turn on ABC," my mother would say to me on the phone. She wasn't talking about a prime-time soap but a sixty-second advertising spot in which a daughter phones her mom or vice versa, by the end of which we were two sentimental saps, promising we'd always remember to call and sobbing and searching for Kleenex.

All I could think was, *Who will I call now?*

The entire funeral was wearing early 1990s black matte jersey skirts and white shirts, stretch wool gabardine jackets and wide-leg trousers or ruched wrap dresses. Jodi zoomed in on the Chanel handbags, and I pointed out some classical two-carat Tiffany & Co. diamond stud earrings, a vintage Bulgari necklace and a Van Cleef & Arpels pin, all pieces my mother had shown or taught me about, which helped me to deflect thoughts about where I was and why I was there.

"Hey, what is your mom wearing?" Jodi asked. Ever since we met when we were fourteen, the thing I liked most and least about Jodi was that she had no filter, and she said anything that came to her mind. In this moment I loved her for it.

AJ hit her hard in the arm. "It's okay," I said, pulling her out the side door, which we were standing next to, and bursting into big belly laughs. I don't know if it was out of grief, out of not knowing what else to do or just a moment of relief in which we could cut through some of the sadness with what would have had my mother laughing too.

Once, after a distant family member's funeral, while driving home, my mother said, "Please dress me in something flattering, something that will hide my middle and my arms, and shoes that will camouflage my big feet."

"Are we allowed to be fully dressed?" I asked. "Didn't Nana Ida once say Jews are buried in basic shrouds?"

"Well, your grandmother can look like Lily Munster if she wants to, but I am reformed, married to a nonpracticing Catholic and being buried in a nonsectarian cemetery when it's time. Dress me in something fashionable and black, please!" At the time, I wanted the conversation over, thinking it funny at first and then scary, but never knowing I'd be making those decisions only a few years later.

I did dress my mom in black—a chic three-quarter-length jacket, Egyptian cotton white long shirt and slim-legged pants with Gucci ballet flats.

"Perfect choice," Jodi said with approval.

Before the service, the rabbi had asked if my brothers and I wanted to see her one more time and if we wanted to put anything into the casket with her. The three of us held hands and our breath as we walked in. David put in a picture he had made her in nursery school of a mother and son facing the sun. Eric offered up his good-luck silver dollar. I knelt down and put in the Jackie Kennedy–style Mikimoto creamy cultured white pearls, which my mom wore throughout the sixties, the ones that made her look like Jackie herself and that she later stored away in favor of my love beads in the seventies. This strand conjured up so many memories: of my parents when they were married, going out for a night on the town; of my mother and my reversal of roles; of how she later changed, becoming stronger and wiser, and how she had grown up with her kids while raising us into adulthood. I thought they were the perfect gift to give back in remembrance of her grace and elegance and the heart, soul and wisdom she passed on over the years.

A few weeks later, I thought about what AJ had said about not breaking down. My grandmother stayed in New York rather than at her home in Florida most of that time. She lost her only daughter and I lost my only mother and we held on tightly to each other. Neither of us was able to give in to the grief, and I was incapable of going to pack up or look through my mother's possessions until three months after the funeral. Manny said it was unbearable to live with all her clothes and mementos around him, waking to them every day and going to sleep with them around him every night. He had hoped she'd come down the stairs to shut off the light or that he'd hear her go into her closet in the morning to try on different pairs of shoes. This was similar to the way I would go to pick up the phone, every night at eleven, not able to get used to her no longer being there, for advice, to tell me to call back after the news or to make plans to go shopping or to swing by her office for lunch.

Since I was her only daughter, my mom left all her jewelry to me. This would be the first time I would look through the small antique dresser that had a marble top, pullout drawer and cabinet, where she kept all her valuable possessions. I already had the art deco engagement watch from when my parents first split. I had the pieces that I was handed in the Ziploc bag and wore most of them every day for the first few months, except for her wedding band from Manny, with an interlocking and continuous branch pattern, accented by small diamonds, which I put away for safekeeping. My mother was not a fan of "showy" jewelry, and I knew that I would find pieces that were either passed down to her from my grandmother when she moved to Florida or from my great-grandmother before she had died. My mother saved everything, and I found styles that had sentimental value and represented different times—a late-sixties magnifying glass pendant, ethnic bangles, a carved jade Buddha with tiny diamonds in the top of the pin, pieces that she was given, that she never wore, that reminded her of all the people she loved and who were part of her history.

As I went through her jewelry, each piece brought forth a precious memory, which defined her life like it would ultimately reflect mine. I called my brothers to come over to choose what they wanted as keepsakes, for when they would get married or have daughters of their own.

When my parents divorced, I always remembered my mom had told me, "Take care of your brothers, keep them safe and stay close together." She repeated it when she went back to work, when she started to date again and when she married Manny. When both Eric and David were in high school, my mother would wake me up in the middle of the night to come pace with her while she waited for one or the other to come home.

"Pacing helps?" I asked. "Are you sure it wouldn't be more productive, say, to call one of their friends or their parents?"

"That would be embarrassing for them," she said.

So we stayed up together eating Häagen-Dazs chocolate chocolate chip, with me following in her footsteps.

"Do either one of my brothers do this with you for me?" I had to know.

"No, of course not. First, you've always called to let me know when you were going to be late, even if it was to whisper that you were about to have sex, making me a little nauseated. Second, they are boys; they have no patience for this."

"So, in essence," I said, "your sons think you are normal, and only I know the truth."

I told my brothers this story while I laid pieces out on her bed, and we laughed for the first time in three months.

David chose the cameo my grandmother had given my mother, which, during the seventies, she used to wear on a wide black velvet ribbon. He had remembered trying to pull it from her neck as a kid. Eric went for the heavy gold link chain bracelet. He recalled how the three charms—14K gold simply and classically styled children's profiles, each representing one of us—used to dangle when she would reach to stop him from leaping, jumping or running after something he thought would be fun to try to catch. We each kept our own name-engraved heads, and when Eric married and had a son, my sister-in-law attached a similar-style charm to the bracelet to signify the birth of my nephew, Robert.

I found a 1950s floral pendant made out of marquis-shaped diamonds surrounding a cultured pearl in white gold that my father had given to my mother when they first got married. It was given during a decade when every woman wore cutout necklines, fit and flare dresses and wanted to look similar and give cocktail parties. It was a piece with no real personality, and after my mother wore it once or twice, it got lost somewhere in a velvet box in the dark recesses of one of her drawers. I took it to a jeweler and had the tiny marquis shapes revamped into a thin stackable eternity band and put the pearl in a tiny Bakelite box that resides next to my parents' photo on my nightstand. Maybe I was still trying to put my parents back together again or maybe I just wanted to re-create a piece of my history that I could wear every day.

I gave my grandmother a simple, comfortable gold bangle, the only piece she wanted and she never took it off.

When David got married and he and my sister-in-law had a daughter—my niece Sammie—I eventually gave her the love beads I had bought my mother in the seventies.

Eric held up an irregularly shaped, almost round medallion made from cracked ceramics on a cord. "Where did this come from, and did Mom actually wear it?" he asked.

"I made it," I said. "I wanted to be more creative than everyone else who was using broken tiles and glass to make their mothers ashtrays in Arts and Crafts."

"You definitely succeeded." He raised his eyebrows at me.

"Really not bad for a five-year-old," David joined in.

"I was thirteen," I said as dryly as I could, breaking the tension of the day for the second time and transporting myself back to my early teenage years, when I acted the same way the first few weeks of sleep-away camp as I had done years before in nursery school.

In nursery school, I cried, hating the idea of being separated from my mother, fearful that something terrible might happen if I was away too long, that I might never see her again. I held on to her leg and didn't let go when she tried to leave me in the classroom. The teacher said it was separation anxiety and that I would be okay if I saw my mother come back at the same time to pick me up every day. It worked, and I finally started releasing my grip.

The letters I wrote home from sleep-away camp approximated the same feelings, perhaps a bit more sarcastically. The first letter home read:

Camp sucks. (Sorry, Mom. I mean stinks.) Remember the bug juice at day camp, which you explained was really just like Kool-Aid? Well, here at Camp Tamakwa, it has real live bugs in it. Okay, they aren't really alive. They are just kind of floating on their backs. I haven't eaten a thing in three days except for M&Ms from the canteen and a box of dry Captain Crunch.

You said I would make a lot of nice new friends. You lied. All the girls have been coming here for years, and they all know each other from home, some place in Long Island called the Five Towns. It's very cliquey, and I don't fit in.

I don't think I can last another day here, but I guess I will have to because I've figured out that it will be about three days before you get this letter and then a day for you to come pick me up. If you absolutely have to, you can wait until the weekend. I mean it, Mom, no longer than that. I started packing, so I will be ready. Please get here soon. By the way, I got stung by a bee and had to stay in the infirmary last night. But don't worry; I didn't die.

Then I went on to tell her I had thirty-seven mosquito bites and that I thought I attracted creepy-crawly things instead of cute guys.

She ignored my plea to pick me up and instead sent me a care package with a new pair of jeans, a bead kit to string bracelets "just in case you make friends," assorted candies and a note that said she would be up on Parents' Weekend. It wasn't until Eric's counselor took me to the lake for a make-out session that she wrote to me that maybe she should come take me home early, but by then I didn't want to leave. She also wrote, *All feels so empty without you. I can't wait to see you again.* And so I went to work on finishing the ashtray pendant to let her know I was thinking of her and sent it with one last note of the summer. *When you pick me up at the bus, please don't get all mushy with me. It's not cool, and all the kids are watching. But don't worry—you can hug me all you want as soon as we get into the car.*

Years later when I had moved into the city and neglected to call her one weekend since I had just started sleeping with a new boyfriend, she phoned me, crying, unable to catch her breath.

"What's wrong?" My heart was pounding down in my feet.

"Why haven't I heard from you? Manny's on a business trip and has been gone all weekend, and I thought we might have gone shopping."

"Just last week, you said I called at the most inopportune times and that I needed to be a little more 'emotionally independent.'"

"I didn't mean this particular weekend!"

It was Sunday, and I invited her to go out to dinner and shopping in SoHo on Monday night. We went to Artwear, which showcased artisan jewelry that was the perfect complement to her all-black wardrobe.

We chose store owner and longtime designer Robert Lee Morris's sculptural gold vermeil and polished sterling silver cuffs, two large rings and a swirl of a pin for her and a few inverted teardrop Ted Meuhling earrings for me.

After my mother passed away, I spent a lot of time watching mothers and daughters, the rivalries, rage and reflections that come in different shapes, sizes and ages.

At the Disney Store, when my niece was three, she pouted and held on tightly to a new blinged-out Princess doll. A tantrum later and a louder "Not this time, honey," my sister-in-law smiled at the other shoppers and, out of sheer embarrassment, gave in. I smiled too; my niece already knew how to work my sister-in-law into getting what she wanted.

When I was five, my appendix almost burst, and I was rushed to the hospital and straight into surgery. I was petrified by the flashing lights and the speed with which they got me onto the gurney. I woke up during the operation, and they had to put ether back over my nose. They kept me for two weeks, the first one spent with me in a blue paper gown, while I figured out how to wear another one as a robe from back to front to hide my rear, which was originally hanging out. The second week ended with my being obsessed with the scar that was the exact size and shape as the one on Frankenstein's head. "It will fade," my mother said as convincingly as possible, but I could not stop looking at it with disbelief. She took me shopping to find something to make me feel pretty. "Maybe a new dress for school, a pair of shoes or a daisy pendant," she had offered. But, as we passed through the accessories department, I saw a tiara sitting in a glass case in the Fifty-ninth Street and Lexington Avenue Bloomingdale's. It was all twinkly and sprinkled with glittering rhinestones and Swarovski crystals, dripping off the sides and decorating the top. It had a metallic sheen that changed from a noble purple to a more royal blue when it moved with the light. I knew it had to be mine. Many years later, I would learn that it was what my mother called "a monstrosity, rivaling only Cher's most ostentatious head-dress." But in the store, she knew she had to get me out without a tantrum and sat me down in a chair and explained, "Oh, honey, there is only one, and they are holding it for a very important duchess from some faraway land. It's amazing that you chose this one. You definitely have royal taste. But let's see if we can find something else worthy of your style and beauty." The sales associates were in awe of the way in which she handled the situation and got into their roles, two of them bringing me a tray of more-toned-down tiara-like headbands, more befitting a five-year-old. When I was adorned in one with just a few seed pearls in a tiny floral design and one single tiny diamanté teardrop surrounded by a delicate scroll on top, my mother held up a mirror and said, "It's you."

She was smart enough to realize that my taste was like

every young girl's, more glitzy than glamorous, and she let me think it was I who decided I was more Grace Kelly than Elizabeth Taylor; however, I do believe that style is inherited and that I developed her knack to choose pieces that would allow me to wear my jewelry rather than have it wear me.

Throughout the years, I continued to notice interactions between mothers and daughters. One day, I watched a mother, around sixty, and daughter, mid-thirties, getting their hair colored. Sipping Diet Cokes with tinfoil wrappers sticking out of their heads, they discussed the daughter's wedding plans and disagreed about everything with the exact same mannerisms. I laughed to myself at their similarities, the ones they couldn't or just didn't want to see. The mother thought the daughter could have used more highlights to brighten up her face. The daughter looked at me and rolled her eyes. I shrugged; I could be of no help to her.

My mother used to hate my hair. The natural gray streak I inherited from my father was "cute for a few years, but by thirty it really needed to go." I kept it until I was thirty-three, when I finally figured out she was right, the year after she died; she never had the chance to say, *I told you so.*

I've come to accept that there are times of the year I will never get used to, like Mother's Day. I put all the extra love and attention into my ninety-six-year-old grandmother. I try to ignore the greeting cards and television commercials, which urge me to buy my mother a gift and suggest jewelry for me, had I become a mother.

For years after my mother died, I listened to my friends who complained about how their mothers still pinched their sides and asked, "Have you gained a little weight?" and criticized the care of their children. These same women also feared their moms' aging and eventually losing them. After all this time, I still don't know what to say: that the pain will grow duller into an ache that will always be there? I don't think they would want to hear that it never goes away. That no matter how old or how many things you have been through, whenever you go to a doctor, have an emergency or someone hurts you, you will always need your mother. That no matter how strong or tough a woman you become, you will always long for her love and her protective words, letting you know that everything will be all right.

One friend compared her feelings surrounding her mother's retirement to Colorado to "grieving her death." She said that her analyst explained, "You are still the child in the crib—crying out for your mother's attention."

I became an adult when my mother went back to work, but I didn't grow up until she passed away, never knowing the meaning of "emotionally independent" until I heard the words, "Your mother is gone." My mother had always called me her "survivor"; she had told me I had compassion and tolerance and the ability to bounce back from the worst of times. If I was her survivor, it was my mom who taught me to be.

So, with empathy, I said to my friend, "Your mother is moving to a warmer climate. There are direct flights. You can help her unpack. You will have holidays and arguments. She might need you more and remember less, but you will *have her!*"

When I look into the mirror, I see lines forming around my eyes. At fifty, only five years younger than my mother was when she passed away, I see her friends—beautiful women like her—who grew up too soon, with children they were too young to raise and husbands like my father, who were still wild. They have gotten facelifts and injections; I have watched them turn more taut and tightened and filled in, fighting against aging. I wish with all my heart that my mom had the chance to fight along with them, and that I had the ability to discuss with her the benefits of Botox and the art of distracting with a few precious colored gems around the face.

Although I think my mother knew it, I might have liked to tell her that I had now realized that she wasn't just a mother but a woman too. That it must have been a bitch to raise three kids with very little help from my dad. I'd like to apologize for never acknowledging that she might have felt just like me—flawed and imperfect, hurt and sometimes angry. I regret that I never thanked her or understood that she was doing the best she could. And that she had done a damn good job. I would tell her that there is never a day that goes by that she is not missed or re-membered. I'd thank her for passing down her style, her specific brand of worrying and nuttiness, her big mushy heart and, especially, for never throwing out the ashtray pendant and for always allowing me to believe I had royal taste.

CHAPTER 8

Career Jewelry

THE NIGHT BEFORE my mother's death, we had spoken about my growing unhappiness as fashion/creative director at *Accessories* magazine, a national trade publication with a focus on jewelry, handbags, shoes, gloves and scarves, where I had I worked for three years.

Prior to that, I freelanced throughout my twenties as a fashion stylist and writer for women's publications and as a columnist about style for the *Village Voice* and New York and Long Island *Newsday*. Although the work brought in a steady income, the overlapping deadlines and long hours had taken over all aspects of my life. When I accepted the position at *Accessories*, I was approaching thirty and longed for a full-time job that came with benefits, vacations that might allow time for socializing with friends and perhaps the opportunity to meet a new man. My role included helping create a more modern image for the magazine and then developing and writing new columns and producing the fashion shoots. But after three years, I found I was putting in even more hours than when I freelanced, and while my publisher said she appreciated this as well as my commitment, we had mounting creative differences about the direction of the look of the covers and fashion photography.

"Start sending out résumés," my mother insisted. "You are too dedicated to be working at a publication that doesn't allow for your talent and vision." My mother's unwavering belief in me kept me going through all the harder decisions in my life.

After she was gone, I realized she had helped me to form the vision she spoke of. I had also been applying what she taught me about style over the years into my work; yet much of what I had incorporated had more to do with the jewelry than the clothes. Some of it was inherited, such as her baroque pearls, or borrowed, like her 1960s Lucite bangles. Another inspiration was watching her identity change with a simple switch of necklace or a ring. Maybe some of it was my own innate "royal taste," my early transformation of trying to twist tinfoil into hoop earrings, my attempts at the sultrier designs of belly chains or when I was enlisted in elementary school to style a production of *My Fair Lady*, and held my breath when Eliza Doolittle came down the stairs in the regal diamond bib neck and tiara I had chosen.

Although my passion for jewelry and fashion was always

present, I hadn't planned on a career in either. I wanted desperately to be a writer. Much of my time at high school was spent filling up spiral-bound notebooks with heartwrenchingly horrible poems about the pathos of failed relationships (mostly written about Cello). With English literature as my major in college, I spent my nights slumped over a Selectric typewriter, drinking Coke, chain-smoking, cranking out more lovelorn verse. I transitioned into short-story writing, the details of which I could never quite change from real-life events. My fiction professor said, "You have a strong voice for first-person narratives. Your dialogue is wonderful. There is heart, and warmth and humor in what you bring to the page. Why not try a few courses in that type of writing?" My mother seemed to be on a similar wavelength. She didn't come out and tell me to give up poetry and fiction; she did, however, gently suggest, "It might be fun to combine your passion for writing with your knack for accessorizing." She noted that while I couldn't change the events of my life in my stories, I could, however, decide on the exact number of bangles to wear with a halter dress and advise on whether it was too flashy to accent a tube top with a wide leather sequin choker.

She had a friend who handled beauty, jewelry and ready-to-wear public relations to whom she could introduce me for a possible summer job. But then I was offered an internship in the subscriptions department of *McCall's* magazine, where my responsibilities consisted of answering phones and filing.

My first article was an assignment received from the nonfiction editor on how to rustproof your car in winter.

"Are you going to write it in iambic pentameter or as a haiku?" my mother teased. Despite her ribbing, this less than riveting five-hundred-word piece became my first "clip."

Six months later, I took her advice (as usual) and became an assistant publicist, producing press kits for clothing and accessories companies and coordinating runway shows, which then led to my career in fashion styling and writing for magazines. I guess sometimes you have to brush off the rust before you can get to the gold.

Although I had not become fully aware of it until I was creatively stunted at *Accessories* and lost my mom, my love for jewelry was always present in the trinkets and treasures I collected at flea markets, the charms I dangled off chains for ankle bracelets and the lanyards I made while in sleep-away camp to give to my best friends. As a fashion stylist, I spent more time trying on earrings and mixing up different textures and metal tones of bracelets in well-known jewelry designers' showrooms than I did choosing the clothes for a photo shoot. Like my mother, I relied on Chanel's approach to dressing for what I chose for the models to wear as well as my own wardrobe. I accented little black dresses with an eclectic mix of jewelry, a cuff on each wrist, creating varied personas and keying into the different moods of women. There were times I knew I wanted to wear layers of necklaces and other times the perfect diamond shooting-star pin. I suspected other women felt this way too.

One of those women was my mom, who had begun to take accessorizing tips from me. Unlike the love bead incident, she wasn't wearing my pieces, but she was taking my suggestions and taking me shopping with her.

The only jewelry category we could never agree upon was earrings. In high school, after a guy named Vinny pierced two more holes in one of my lobes and one in the other for an "asymmetrical look" with a sewing needle and ice, she ran for the alcohol swabs and canceled an outing to Bloomingdale's. When heavy ethnic-inspired styles made a comeback, she voiced her concern that "they would get caught on a sweater and rip my ears to shreds." She had a sense for the dramatic, although I still make sure I take off my earrings (even studs) before I pull any piece of clothing over my head. During the early 1990s when "shoulder dusters" showed up on every runway and in every magazine, I complained about how a pair I bought had dipped into my drink and got hooked on the glass while I was trying to make an impression with a handsome date. Instead of giving me an all-knowing look, my mom said, "It sounds like a charming moment." She tried hard not to be sarcastic about my lobes when my love life was at stake.

After my mother's funeral, I took a week off from work. Shortly after returning, I told my publisher I was giving my two-week notice. I knew if we kept butting heads about the magazine's creative content, we would lose the mutual respect we had for each other. I wanted to walk away while we were still on good terms. "You are having a reaction to your mom's death. It's totally normal. Take some time to think about it, and if you feel the same way in three weeks, we can talk about it again," my publisher advised.

"We are putting off the inevitable," I asserted. It was the first time in my life that I was not afraid to be jobless and completely on my own. My publisher went to management and got me what amounted to two months' severance to tide me over and continued to assign freelance stories to me.

A month after I left *Accessories*, I was hired as a wardrobe stylist for HBO for its downtown division that produced Comedy Central programming. I also landed freelance gigs at MTV dressing VJs and at Showtime for promo segments. I had no idea what I was doing, but I liked the change to styling real people—as opposed to models—who needed to move in their clothes and not have their necklaces safety pinned in the back in case they decided to turn around. I taught myself different beading techniques for necklaces for the women comics and hosts I was styling. The writers, producers and directors began to buy various pieces I made for their girlfriends and wives.

I spent my downtime on set doodling ring designs— hearts and scroll and rose and thorn patterns that had both a Victorian and tattoo-inspired feeling. When a friend who owned a sterling silver company came by to drop off some

of the week with the collection and she would introduce me to her boss, who wound up placing an order that same day. When it came to my career, I felt I was surrounded by luck and serendipity (very dissimilar to the way I felt about the rest of my life). I also felt that my mom was smiling at me.

My jewelry line was a mix of my favorite elements: the delicate and openwork motifs found in vintage lace and embroidery patterns, such as scrolls, vines, leaves and floral motifs, and architectural designs of wrought iron and mosaic-tile patterns. It also sold to Nordstrom stores, smaller specialty fashion and jewelry stores and major catalog companies.

The following year, while I was traveling throughout Italy for inspiration, a chic, well-dressed woman introduced herself to me on the boat going from Venice to Murano, where I was going to see the glass factories. She pointed to my necklace. "You are wearing my favorite designer," she said, lifting up a sleeve on her leather jacket to reveal one of my bracelet designs. "I buy all my Bethany B. pieces in the Beverly Hills Barneys."

"I'm Beth." I felt myself go red.

"Oh my God, you're famous." It was definitely "my fifteen minutes." What she couldn't have known was that Barneys had filed to operate in chapter eleven and had not paid me on my past four deliveries. Financially it was a big hit to take when counting on these payments to produce my new orders with other stores. I pressed on for three more years of eighteen-hour days and massive amounts of caffeine, determined to make it work. Although I had begun to make a recognizable name for the company, like most independent designers, I had accumulated debt and kept pouring more money into sample collections, trade shows and branding. I had to admit to myself that I didn't have the financial resources to grow the business.

I finally decided to close my company when approached by two different sterling silver manufacturers to design for them on a contract basis. It kept gnawing at me that I had failed. But then I thought about what my mother would have said. She would have pointed out the positives of my experience. All around me I felt her support and unconditional faith in me, which guided me into the next phase of my career.

I had the wonderful opportunity to work on designs for Cynthia Rowley's jewelry licensee through one company and created two sterling silver collections for the Betsey Johnson stores through the other company. I also helped launch the Judith Ripka 18K gold and sterling silver line, and designed for other various well-known, established jewelry firms.

This gave me the impetus to open my own consulting company in 2002 and design, merchandise and work on business plans, branding and marketing for both large and small jewelry companies. I also continued to create one-of-a-kind pieces for private clients under the Bethany B. name.

It took a while to get there, but I finally grasped the full scope of how my mother's influence helped me to understand my intimate relationship with jewelry and all the facets that went into shaping my career. I am sure she would have been proud. I know she is looking down to make sure that I still "take one piece off before leaving the house" and that I also take my earrings off before I pull my sweater off over my head.

CHAPTER 9

The Ring That Got Away

R AY WAS MY only one-night stand, although he'd never seen it that way. Whenever I would reminisce, he'd ramble off the "real" definition to prove me wrong.

"You meet someone, take them home or to your car (depending on age and living situation), have sex and then you never see the person again, or if you bump into them, you both act like it's no big deal or it never happened. I seriously hope you are seeing the irony in what you are saying about us."

"Stop getting all defensive." I waved my hand, brushing it off with a straight face.

"I've been in your life . . . forever." He got up and walked around.

"More like in and out of it." I poked at him.

"And we knew each other for a while before having sex," he interjected.

"Yes, well, *that* I remember. It took me, what, three months to get you home with me."

"Exactly. That's what I just said." He mock-kicked me in the butt.

I could tease Ray all I wanted, but I was never good at casual sex, not with Ray, not with anyone before or since. Cello was my first, and it took six years to fully get over him. There was AJ in high school and part of college, and then we became best friends. Later, whenever I had truly steamy sex, I thought it was love and turned it into a lengthy and angst-y romance as was the case with Liam, spending more time getting over the breakup and obsessing over what went wrong than I did in the actual relationship. My other scenario was turning my exes into best friends who helped me out rigging up stereos, cleaning air-conditioning filters and killing bugs. More important, they gave me advice on other men. They were more reliable figuring out their own gender than my mother, grandmother or women friends.

Ray might have started out as a one-nighter, but he ironically turned into the guy who wanted to stick around and build a life together, although it took twelve years after we first met for him to figure this out, and not in a *When Harry Met Sally* friends-but-we-are-really-meant-for-each-other way. It was more like a three-different-relationships-with-one-guy plotline, evoking feelings in me that ranged from confused to conflicted to comforted.

I was twenty-one the first time around. I spotted him on a dance floor, took him home, had hot lusty all-night sex, which over the course of the following five months he never asked me to do again (thus making me want him even more). Two years later I bumped into him, and we got involved in an intense yearlong relationship, which he broke off, turning him into the second guy I fell in love with who eventually placed a ring on someone else's finger. This time it was a turn-of-the-century setting with a blue sapphire center and two European cut diamonds on each side—small, pretty, tasteful, a type of ring I might have worn, if I'd been asked.

Ray and I started talking again after not being in touch for eight years, around two months before my mother passed away. He called to tell me he was divorced with two young kids.

When I teased him about our earlier years, I got *the definition*, which ended with, "I am the exact opposite of a one-night stand. I am the goddamn one that got away."

"Well, no. You left, and now you're back." I climbed into his lap and curled into his chest.

Ray mouthed, *I'm here*, as we were taking our seats. I had not broken down or cried since the nurses in the hospital told me it was time to go in and say my final good-bye to my mother.

I could hug my grandmother and brothers to comfort them but could not let anyone hold me—not my family, not AJ, not my stepfather or even my father, who tried for the first time in years.

And then Ray walked in.

He was a bit beefier than I remembered, still handsome with his full head of shiny black hair. He was wearing a dark suit, which I'd never seen him in before. After the funeral service, he walked past the crowd of my mother's friends talking and offering condolences, right up to me and wrapped me up in his arms. As soon as he pulled me in closer and I could feel his breath on my neck, the tears came and wouldn't stop. I was sobbing and slobbering all over his suit, wiping my nose with my sleeve while my mascara was running onto his shirt. The more I cried, the tighter he held me. I felt protected and cared for, and I didn't want to let go of Ray or my mother; I wanted to be lost in this feeling instead of feeling the unbearable loss.

My mother, who had liked Ray best of all my boyfriends, said he was "mush behind his facade of machismo." They watched old movies together. He would whip up great pasta. They would go on walks with my stepfather and the dog and watch football with my brothers when they came home from school. My favorite memories of Ray and my mom were of them dancing around the house together, with him teaching her how to Latin hustle and her teaching him how to salsa, reminding me of when Ray and I first met.

It was 1981, and the DJ was mixing the pulsating sounds of Teena Marie with earlier songs by Evelyn "Champagne" King and Cheryl Lynn. I was dancing off to the side, dressed in a draped purple silk halter top and Fiorucci jeans that were so tight I had to lie on my bed and use a hanger to pull the zipper up. I accented the look with large thin gold hoop earrings and a chain I fastened around my waist, made from a long 14K gold necklace my grandmother gave me, which I redesigned with tiny gold nuggets, after taking a beading class. The chain, which I never took off, fell somewhere between my navel and my hips and sometimes slid over my pants when I danced. AJ said it was hot. My mother asked if I was taking up belly dancing as a side career, and all my friends asked me to make them one. The week before, when Ray had come up behind me, under the flashing neon lights flickering in time with the music, he'd slipped his fingers underneath the chain, lightly tickling my bare skin. He'd gently pulled me closer to him, moving my hips in time with his. It was our only dance together that night. I dragged AJ with me the next week in hopes of seeing Ray again.

Although disco wasn't really AJ's thing, meeting women was, and he was cute enough and had enough technique to meet an endless supply of girls who would buy him drinks and take him home with them. We were each other's wing "men" before the term was even coined. I had desperately wanted to move into the city after we'd left Boston University, but rents were high and my salary as assistant editor for a women's magazine was low, so I took my father up on his offer to rent an apartment he owned in a complex in Edgewater, right below Fort Lee, long before the area had been completely developed. AJ said it was a great deal. It was a huge studio with separate kitchen and dressing room, had a wraparound terrace that overlooked the Hudson and had an amazing view of the New York skyline. I only had to cover the maintenance, and it was twenty minutes into the city where I would go to dance on weekends.

Since I'd dropped ballet for modern jazz when I was in grade school, dancing had given me a sense of freedom and a release, first from my shyness and then from the more troubling times of my father's infidelities and my parents' divorce. I was a go-go girl in camp and did the frug and the twist during the sixties and then the monkey and pony through the bubble-gum era of my adolescent years. During high school, I learned how to do the bump to Barry White, while my mother taught me the merengue and cha-cha in our living room and my grandmother showed me the Lindy and Charleston. When *Saturday Night Fever* came out, I hustled myself into clubs with a fake ID and danced with the guys who tried to emulate John Travolta, using more hair spray than their female counterparts and wearing polyester fabrics that stuck to them under the sparkle of the silvery disco balls. While I was in college in Boston, managers from strip joints in the section called the Combat Zone (then akin to the "old" Forty-second Street in NYC) canvassed the clubs for young girls and propositioned me. "You will have protection, you can wear a bikini top and it's up to you if you want to take it off or not." As flattering as the offer was, I turned them down, in favor of keeping my clothes on and dropping them in a tub of RIT dye, pure magic for a poor college girl to create new outfits each week. I turned oversized Hanes T-shirts into vivid turquoise tunics and transformed slinky off-the-shoulder dresses I found at forty percent–off sales into red-hot numbers that I wore with platform heels, gold bangles, mesh chokers and, always, the belly chain. I met Ray the summer I came home from Boston on ladies' night at one of the more crowded clubs on Route 46 in New Jersey to practice for the weekends in Manhattan, when I went to the more glamorous clubs such as Odeon and Area.

Ray had the shifty, rugged looks of a modern-day Clark Gable, black hair, black eyes that softened when he smiled, broad shoulders and a manlier build than most of the guys I was used to dancing with. He led me to the middle of the crowded floor, raising my hands in his over our heads, and spun me out and then into him, his fingers outlining and gliding down my waist, gently letting me out and firmly pulling me back. I could feel his muscular arms beneath his billowy shirt with tunic collar, which he wore with baggy trousers and lace-up black Capezio dance shoes. And, I could follow him; he got lost in the words and music like I did, and he moved my hips in time with his as the DJ spun 1970s disco favorite "Dance Turned into Romance" effortlessly into "Midnight Love Affair." When Rod Stewart's 1978 hit "Da Ya Think I'm Sexy" came on, he said, "You've got bad hips, baby," his voice deep and crackling with sex appeal. "And an even badder sense of style." I think it was the first time he had spoken to me.

AJ said, "That's one hell of a line."

"Who cares? He's the hottest guy I've ever met. I want to take him home with me."

"Wait. Not sure that's such a good idea. You've never done that before."

"Well, I am about to start."

"Maybe not. He just walked out the door with that beautiful waitress I was talking to. She must have just got off work." I was crushed.

It took four more weeks of dancing with him and four brightly dyed outfits before Ray went home with me. All I knew about him was his name, that he grew up in Hawthorne, New Jersey, that he finished college, taking night courses while helping support his mother after his dad left her two years earlier. He had two brothers, one younger and one older, who also hung out at the club.

Once back in my house, he picked up my notebooks of poems and asked if he could read them; I pulled them away. I told him I'd gone to high school in Fort Lee and that my parents had been divorced for many years. I began nervously chatting up a storm, which stopped when he started kissing the back of my neck while telling me that I had the most beautiful eyes and that he loved dancing with me. Then he took me firmly in his arms, gently laying me down on my couch, tenderly kissing me, moving as he did to the music with confidence and abandon. I had never had sex that many times in one night and got goose bumps the next morning just thinking about doing it again. We stayed in bed late and went to a diner to have lunch. When he was leaving, he said, "See you next Thursday night," and winked at me.

I repeated it to AJ quizzically. "'See you next Thursday'? What's that? We did it like seven times. Why doesn't he want to see me again?"

"I thought you just wanted to have sex with him?"

"I did, and now I want to again."

"He's not the guy for you. You had a good time. So leave it at that. If you can't, then this wasn't a great choice for you."

That was the understatement to beat all. I saw Ray five more times. He danced with me on all those nights, sometimes lifting my hair and kissing my neck, complimenting me, but he never asked me to go home again. "Hit and Run Lover" was playing the last time I saw him, and then he just stopped coming to the club. A few months later, one of his friends told me he started dating a woman named Tina, whom I'd met a few times. She was five years older than he was and already had a three-year-old daughter and an ex-husband. I couldn't stop thinking about him or that night, going over in my mind what I had done wrong.

"You never asked me again," Ray said almost two years

later when I ran into him at a mutual friend's house. "I always wanted to be with you, but you seemed aloof and distant, different from when we had been together. I always wondered why," he continued.

"Because I was scared to ask. Because you kept dancing with me and going home with other women," I told him. "Because I had never gone home with someone I hardly knew before. I wasn't distant—I was embarrassed and wanted you to be the one to ask me."

"I thought you just did it for fun and then lost interest. We should have talked about it." He felt around for my belly chain, sliding his fingers under it next to my skin, and told me he was glad to see me again. Besides the time I'd been with him at my house, I don't think I'd ever seen him in the light of day. He was wearing a gray T-shirt, jeans and sneakers, and he looked even sexier in these clothes than the horrible Deney Terrio ensembles that he and all the other guys used to wear to the clubs.

This time I wasn't letting him leave without taking my phone number. "A first date," he teased me, "one in which you talk to me and let me read your poetry."

"Well, one in which we talk, at least."

I found out that he had broken up with Tina a few months before. I'd learned more about him in a week than I had known about him in all those months I spent at the club with him. We danced at my house to our old favorites as I imitated him, all his moves, and repeated his old lines to him, making him crack up and ask, "Did I really do/say that?" We had both grown up. He told me that he had reconnected with his father and made peace with his stepmother, that he still took care of his mother financially, that one of his brothers was a cop and the other one was a musician. We went to see him perform at different places in New Jersey and the city. He knew how to whip up quick dinners from leftovers and make pasta from scratch. I met his mother, who told him she thought I had an incredible heart and that she wanted me as her daughter-in-law. Ray was the first guy who spooned with me, never letting go, making the nights we spent together feel safe and sensual at the same time. He was proud of me when I started writing about fashion and style and producing fashion shoots for women's and lifestyle magazines. He loved hearing about my days at work, and I couldn't wait to get home to tell him everything. He was climbing the ranks of a major company, working in sales and then marketing, but he felt stuck and wasn't sure about what he wanted to do. We were twenty-three. I thought he had time to decide. He thought I had gone much farther than he had.

After almost a year of calm and finally being secure in a relationship, a feeling I had not known through the many years of ups and downs with Cello, Ray came to pick me up, looking sadder than I'd ever seen and acting more timid than I'd known him to be.

"What's wrong?" My feet went numb.

"I love you, but we are from such different worlds," he

blurted out, sitting on a chair far away from me rather than curled up close to me on the couch. That was a new one. Or was it? Hadn't Cello loved me but couldn't be with me? Hadn't all the guys I'd known, since Victor took back his ring, found a reason why they couldn't be with me? Even my junior high school boyfriends had done that. My love life always felt like a game of spin the bottle, the bottle stopping on someone else. I couldn't breathe and felt faint listening to Ray. It was the same feeling as when you stand up too quickly and your blood pressure drops, putting you off balance with the sense that things are about to go dark.

"This isn't easy for me," Ray said.

"Hey. Stop talking about what it's doing to you. Tell me straight out."

"I just did. You are so smart, and you are simplifying our relationship. It's more complicated, not black and white."

I'd gone blank by this time. It was all becoming an excuse to me. He added, "You are on track to have the career you want; you are saving for an apartment in the city. You are gorgeous, smart and charming, although God knows why you don't see it. I will bring you down, and you will wind up hating me."

"Don't tell me how I feel," I said. He started to cry, and I pushed him out the door. I couldn't listen anymore.

I said to my mother, "Don't give me that line about how I will find someone else more worthy of me." I was shaking and sobbing and yelling at her all at the same time.

"I wasn't going to. Ray is the last good man on the planet. I doubt you'll find anyone else better than him," she gently teased, and started to braid my hair as she did when I was younger to calm me down.

"Okay—the real truth—this one is heartbreaking," she said. "He was a good guy, unlike the other schmuck, Cello, who couldn't think for himself. But Ray is right. I know you don't want to hear it right now, but you are going in totally different directions, and, as much as you love each other, he isn't the one for you."

"Again?"

"It will happen."

I put my hand over her mouth to stop the pep talk. "Just let me cry it out."

Ray wound up getting married to a woman named Cheryl, having two kids, a boy and a girl, one right after the other. I was devastated when I heard and more so after I saw her ring, when I ran into them in the food court at the Garden State Mall. I had a few short-term relationships, each one lasting a year or less. Then I met Jay and after him, Liam.

It wasn't until eight years after our breakup that AJ ran into Ray, found out he was divorced and gave him my number just around the time Liam and I broke up.

He came back into my life first as a friend when I lost my mother, both of us recovering from our own traumas. I could feel the old chemistry stirring, but it felt best to take it slowly.

"I was an idiot back then. I loved you so much but let you go. I wound up marrying Cheryl because I thought we grew up the same way and it felt like it would be right. But it went bad and we fought constantly, right after we had our first kid. I love both my children and have joint custody, but I'm so glad to be out of that relationship." He continued. "I thought we'd be able to grow together, and instead we grew so far apart. And I never stopped thinking about you."

The words I so wanted to hear when I was in my twenties didn't move me all these years later, even though being with Ray felt natural and I felt safer with him than with any other guy I'd ever known.

After six months of hanging out with Ray, with him giving me space, yet being there for me and waiting patiently for me to turn our relationship from platonic back into the passionate sexuality we shared, I could not do it. I could not bring myself to sleep with him.

"Now do you see the irony?" He tried to act nonchalant.

He was my one-night stand, the man I felt too strongly about to sleep with again for fear of leading him to think we had a future together. He had come back, ready to give me the life I had so wanted all those years before. But I had moved on. I was already flirting with one of the actors/comedians I met at the job I took as a wardrobe stylist at MTV after my mother died. Both my mother and Ray had been right about our relationship; at that time, however, I was too young, too impulsive and living too much in the moment to see it. We had gone in different directions, and in growing up, I seemed to grow out of Ray. As my mom had said, "This one was heartbreaking." I still felt the same sense of comfort and closeness that comes from sharing a history, but it was not the basis for a long-term commitment, though I wished and even tried at one point to make myself believe it could be.

It wasn't until three years later that Ray told me he had a ring picked out—an Edwardian platinum ring with smaller diamonds surrounding an antique cut center stone—and a dream of what our lives could be.

But ever since we met, our timing was off. We felt differently about each other at separate moments in our lives and had to accept it. Once we made our peace with the past, Ray became one of my closest friends. He never really did "get away." Still in my life, he is one of the best men I know.

CHAPTER 10

Talisman Jewelry

I HAD CONVINCED MYSELF that Nick Testino and I were destined to be together from the moment he showed up in the MTV wardrobe room with his unruly brown hair, his baggy gray sweatshirt and his worn jeans that hung in all the wrong places. I thought we were fated because I was reconsidering my "type" (i.e., men who didn't stick around), and upon immediately finding him to be cocky and full of himself, I thought, *This is the new guy for me.* It was definitely not the instant physical chemistry I'd had with Liam or the first time with Ray, but it was a different kind: If there had been a window in my office/dressing room, I'd have thrown him out immediately.

Throughout my life, I'd been recasting myself in movies and had always banked on black and white with a happy ending. At this stage, it wasn't far-fetched for me to compare our initial reaction to some of my favorite leads in 1940s romantic comedies who bantered, argued, drove each other crazy and eventually realized they were meant to be together. His sense of timing was pitch-perfect. Standing there in his Calvin Klein skivvies, on our second day working together, he blurted out, "You are aware that you're bossy and somewhat of a bitch" while I was laying out his wardrobe. I pushed him out the room, into the hallway, and demanded, "Get over it and into these." I threw pants at him and wrapped it up with, "Don't give me any more shit." So Nick was not as charming as Cary Grant and I was definitely not as self-possessed as Irene Dunne. He was more like the guy who snapped my training bra straps in fifth grade and, after I stuck my tongue at him, kissed me in the school yard.

I'd been given Nick's measurements and reels of his old interview shows to watch before he arrived at MTV as guest host on one of the shows I was working on as wardrobe stylist. He was dark like Cello and Ray, yet taller and lankier with long gorilla limbs that worked for physical comedy and features that were kind of cockeyed—all of which made for an offhandedly sexy and attractive package. He was a magnetic contrast of boyish mischievousness and machismo. And he was funny: smart, dark and wickedly funny.

At the studio, I had been warned by some of the guys—writers and directors—that he was a handful. After seeing me with hard-to-handle talent (meaning other comics with whom we worked), they realized I could hold my own if I was prepared in advance. Plus they longed for a little tension on the set. Prior to his arrival, they were warming me up like a boxer going into the ring. "Be light on your feet. Don't let him see what's coming. Try and get the first jab in; if he does, come back quickly." One of the guys was even rubbing my shoulders like before a sparring match. I'd also heard he was a major flirt and not politically correct with his humor. But I felt I had the upper hand because much of our time together was spent with his pants off and my holding a steamer, hot iron or scissors.

On the third day he asked, "So, do you want to go out for drinks after the taping tonight?"

"Maybe. If you change your outfit," I said.

"Don't waste any time on tact," he said. He sat down on the floor next to me where I was folding clothes that had come back from the laundry, and we wound up talking for four hours over Coke and chips, discussing everything from Sartre to the hazards of wearing stripes on screen. I found out that he'd grown up in the city and, like every good New Yorker, hated living in Los Angeles. He'd started out working comedy clubs after college and did everything from TV to Broadway plays; he felt his career was like a train wreck, much in the way I thought about my relationships. He thought "the airlines should spend more money on rivets to hold the aircraft together rather than buying peanuts, which no one gets a hankering for at thirty-five thousand feet. They'd rather be lulled into thinking the plane will land."

He believed that Catholicism taught "people not to sin in life and then, oh what a party they will have after they are dead." He also believed that the only way to meet people in LA was "to smile at them from your car." Listening to him disarmed me. He was much more down to earth and approachable than the guys had led me to believe. I told him about my discomfort with flying—that I was okay on nonstop, but that if I had to land and take off twice for one trip, I freaked. I confessed I truly believed that if someone told me flying was safer than driving, I would land and then have a bad feeling about getting into a car. And if anyone ever said it was a one in a million chance, the odds were that *one* would happen. Nick nodded his head in understanding the whole time while other friends, boyfriends and family had always looked at me as if I were a lunatic.

"Ever feel like irony is having its way with you?" he asked. "Listening to you makes life feel manageable and sane." Then he said, "You are the coolest woman I've met in a long time. I'd like to hang out with you for the rest of my stay and in two months when I return."

I felt a rush of excitement. For the first time since he arrived, I was at a loss for words. The next day, when I saw him walk in with a Kelly green silk shirt, I insisted that we go shopping.

"You can't go around looking like you just stepped off the set of *Jack and the Beanstalk* and you have been cast as the stalk."

I found out that the reason his personal style was so horrifying was because it wasn't his style at all—he was just throwing together what his last wardrobe stylist had procured for him. He was a guy and an actor/comedian: giveaways from his favorite comedy clubs and cable channels were an acceptable form of dress. I found jeans that accentuated his waist and cute butt, and sweaters with T-shirts underneath that hinted at broader shoulders and a V-shape. I got him to cut his hair and, at the stylist's suggestion, to straighten it to bring out his large brown eyes. "The last time I was styled this much, I had a bit part as the drug dealer in an episode of *Miami Vice*."

"God, you're old," I said, and he threw a stack of straws at me.

The next time he came to town, it was New Year's Eve. I had already made plans with Ray to have a quiet dinner at my house. Yet, by this time, I had figured out that Ray and I would not wind up together. This was all confirmed for me when Nick called at nine p.m. "So, do you want to catch the midnight showing of *Schindler's List* with me?"

"I'll call you right back," I said. His voice mail picked up. I left a message. "What better way of ringing in the new year than with a three-and-a-half-hour film, watching people who have way bigger problems than we do?"

I then missed his next call, and he left this message for me: "How cool is it to be able to see a movie on New Year's more depressing than your own life?" When Nick called back and we actually talked, he said, "We are twins separated at birth."

I told him I was sorry I already had plans. But I was drawn to Nick and his desire to see long, intensely sad movies instead of to join in fake festivities. He didn't make resolutions and was honest, realistic and maybe just slightly depressed, but he could also be self-deprecating and find humor in almost anything.

But what truly confirmed my original belief about our being a perfect fit was when he told me his birthday, which was the same date that my mother had passed away. That was when I knew without a doubt that we were soul mates.

When I told my grandmother about all of this, she didn't sound overjoyed and instead said, "I remember him in cheesy sitcoms. I don't think there was a TV show he ever appeared on that wasn't canceled or didn't cancel him. He's no big whoop."

She was in a huff and added, "The guy with the pretty *punim* who came back and took care of you—he's the one you should be with!"

"Punim?" I asked.

"Oh, Bethy," she said with a sigh, calling me by the name she saved for when she was really disappointed in me. "It means face. You know less Yiddish than half the *goyisha* comedians you work with. Here is a man who loves you and with whom you wanted to run away when you were in your twenties, and now you want to give him up for someone you hardly know."

"But Nan, what about Nick's birthday?" I couldn't believe she didn't get it. "Maybe Mom has sent me someone she knows is perfect for me." I was now not only superstitious; I had morphed into a cross between Dionne Warwick and Shirley MacLaine.

"The birthday is a coincidence. Trust me. Your mother would not be sending you a second-rate TV star."

"Comedic actor and talk show host," I corrected her.

"Semantics. But sweetie, I don't think you've thought this out. Let's say it all works. How will you be able to celebrate his birthday when you will also be thinking about your mom not being here?" She had a point, but right then and there I wanted to know why my grandmother, of Russian heritage and raised a conservative Jew, had not one ounce of superstition in her. Yes, she had become more laid-back about religion after my mom, her only daughter, married an Italian Catholic, her granddaughter (me) went out with guys she deemed "mobsters or IRA," one of her grandsons (Eric) could no longer be buried in a Jewish cemetery after getting a tattoo and her other grandson (David) married a Christian from the "backwaters of Indiana," where a reverend, not unlike Jimmy Swaggart, performed the ceremony.

But as far as anything that could be misconstrued as superstitious, her fallback line was "It's an old wives' tale," and everything that could be seen as predestined was "a complete accident." The only thing that gave her cultural upbringing away was her belief in chicken soup as a cure. But as always, she stood behind what I wanted and said, "Let's hope this one will wind up in marriage." She left out her usual punch line, "While I'm still here to see it," because she knew it scared me too much to think about losing her as we had my mother.

After Nick had been back in LA for a month, he sent me a round-trip ticket with a note: *I hope the plane doesn't crash.* He remembered our first night's conversation and seemed to be wooing me with his understanding of what he called my *mishagosh*. Nana Ida was right. These guys knew more Yiddish phrases than I would ever pick up, and Nick had definitely gotten to know me.

"What do you mean you booked a hotel?" he asked. "That's ridiculous. I already know from hanging out with you at your place, that you turn on the water so I won't hear you pee. I also know that, for some incomprehensible reason, you lock the bathroom door when you put on makeup or brush your teeth. God forbid I should see you rinse or put on mascara. Stop the shenanigans. You are staying with me."

I loved that he had figured this all out and still wanted to be with me.

My first night's outfit, which was decided upon after nine wardrobe changes, included an ever so slightly cropped sand-colored cotton sweater, which just grazed the top of my skirt and showed off my new belly chain, a small bezel-set diamond chain that Nick loved to put his fingers between and roll up and down against my skin while he talked to me, sort of like Ray did, while dancing all those years ago. I also wore high Doc Martens boots and black opaque tights.

"Bend over," said Nick, who had not even tried to kiss me. *Now we are getting somewhere,* I thought. Not quite the romantic lead-in, but at least it smacked of sex.

"Now try to pick this up." He dropped a piece of copier paper on the floor. "There is no room for margin of error in that skirt. You'd better stand or sit with your legs tightly crossed. If you drop anything, come and get me."

"Aww, the sarcastic SOB I first met." He tackled me.

The next day, we bonded over two of our favorite movies (the original *Manchurian Candidate* and *Diabolique*) and favorite foods (Nathan's French fries and Brooklyn-style egg creams), while we were sitting in an organic, tofu-imitation-everything café. On Venice Beach, he bought me a black rubber bracelet for fifty cents. "It's what all the kids are wearing," he said, and then had an idea. He had seen a German jewelry designer who mixed rubber, metal and diamonds, and he took me to the nearest jewelry store to have a small white diamond set in the center of the bracelet. It became my favorite piece, which I never took off, except when I'd remove a sweater or jacket too quickly and it would ping across the room. The rubber had a lot of spring in it and could wind up anywhere—sort of like Nick.

Early on, I found out that he slept around, a lot; he didn't pass up anyone, from the craft service girls to the waitresses at comedy clubs across the entire United States, to actresses and women he met on airplanes. The list went on. It seemed that the only person on the planet that Nick had not had sex with was me.

I had hoped that during the trip to LA, he would finally make some sort of attempt to jump my bones. I had never known a guy this long without a little passionate kissing or some sort of foreplay. Even the security guards in Dublin Airport had copped more of a feel.

But I'd started seeing a therapist, who said that it was important after what I had "gone through" to take it slow and get to know someone and trust the person first. Although she was talking specifically about the recent loss of my mom, I had taken it to mean that with my track record, after being dumped by Jay and Liam, after my mom died, after I'd grown out of the relationship I had at twenty-three, after I got a rash from being a bridesmaid in scratchy polyester at my brother David's wedding—or maybe it was just that I got hives due to the younger of my two brothers getting married first—it might be wise not to jump into any new circumstances too fast, which could screw me up more. I was sure she was right about the whole waiting bit . . . but it had been long enough, and it was time to get Nick into bed.

And so I slipped into my little French lace teddy and boy shorts. Nick, shirtless, in his black Calvin's that I met him in, perhaps not the same exact pair but the same style, snuggled up against my back, cuddling and spooning and snoring and sweating all over me and *sleeping* the whole night until eleven a.m. the next day, when he jumped into the shower and proceeded to go downstairs to make me French toast.

"Don't want any." I pushed the plate away. Instead, I opted for breakfast conversation. "So, do you find me sexually repulsive or what?" It came out of my mouth before I had the chance to revise or tweak it into something just a tad more witty, although it made him laugh loudly and almost spit his coffee out of his mouth.

Once I'd said it, I couldn't stop. "Well?"

"A better intro might have been, 'I noticed that we slept together without having sex. I am feeling a little weird about this and was wondering if we could talk about it?'"

"Don't rewrite my dialogue after you've perspired on me all night." My hormones were raging and I was seriously confused about men. Most of them just wanted to get laid, and here was Nick, sending me plane tickets and wanting me to stay at his house . . . to sleep.

"I am trying to help you see yourself. You are the opposite of repulsive—beautiful, witty, charming and real. The fact that you don't know this is scary enough. The fact that you would go to the lowest common denominator means you are hearing only the bad."

All that I could think of in the moment was to once again default to *When Harry Met Sally*, the line when Meg Ryan asks Billy Crystal, "So you're saying that a man can be friends with a woman he finds unattractive?" And he replies, "No. You pretty much want to nail 'em too."

"I am attracted to you. But I don't want to be in a romantic relationship. We got close really quickly, and we are already involved. If we have sex, it will get intense and all complicated, and it won't last," Nick offered.

This was a new one. I figured it was hard to tell someone so close to you, *I am not and never will be hot for you.* I put him in this position. Or was it really true? It would be fate, but a twisted fate in which I would never have a physical relationship with the guy I was destined to be with.

When I got moody and quiet, he said, "We did talk about it that first week." I vaguely remembered Nick saying he did not believe in marriage, having children or anything conventional like that. Like most thirty-three-year-olds who were still optimistic and tragically hopeful about love, I thought I'd be the one who could change him.

Over the next year he sent funny postcards just to say hi or to cheer me up when I was sick, talked me through having to put my dog to sleep, my grandmother's getting a horrible case of pneumonia and when I had some pangs of sibling envy when David called to tell me his wife was pregnant. I was there for him during pilot season, when his stepfather was diagnosed with cancer and when his sister was divorcing her husband and falling apart. I met him for awards dinners, club dates, events in Seattle, Florida, San Diego, Chicago,

Boston, DC and, of course, New York and LA. He invited me to San Francisco for my birthday and had his travel agent book the flight for the first time without telling her the parameters: direct flights only! It took me twelve hours and two stops to get there. "First you try and get me over my insecurities about men by not having sex with me, and now you try to get me over my lingering doubts about flying by sending me through Oshkosh to get to you. What's next?"

I met him in DC where he bought me a Florentine textured dog tag on a long chain with the inscription *Fearless* on it. It was beautiful. I then ate bad salmon, which gave me the worst case of the runs; yet he didn't let me go down the hallway in the hotel to the ladies' room. No. He wanted me to know it was okay to be around guys who cared about me when I was sick. "So you go to the lobby while I use the bathroom here," I said, feeling a little faint.

"No chance." In many ways, he let me know it was okay to be human, vulnerable and real in front of men, which made me feel closer to him. I felt the fish incident would squelch any chance, however minute, we had for a sex life. Plus, everything with him was a shock to the system, kind of like the exposure therapy I had to endure before getting onto the plane.

Rachel was the first long-term therapist I had seen, and she still believed my sexless relationship with Nick was good. She said, "It's probably the healthiest relationship you ever had with a man besides your friend AJ."

"Why?" I challenged. I thought I might very well be see-ing the worst therapist in the city where the ratio of shrinks to patients was much more promising than men to women. But I listened. "Because in the past, every time you fell in love, it was based on sex. And now you've been more inti-mately involved without sleeping together."

There was something oddly fatalistic in the fact that I could never get the man I wanted to want me back at the same time.

"Fate. Schmate," my grandmother said. "It's nonsense. You always chose the wrong men. And you are doing it again. It's time to move on."

Rachel said that I had either stayed too long in relation-ships or chosen guys stunted in their ability to love me at the time I loved them. She did not feel that Nick was one of these men. Two weeks later, she told me she had received a research grant she'd wanted and was shifting her practice around and would be seeing fewer patients.

"Let me guess. I will be one of those patients you stop seeing?"

"Yes, but you've done hard work, and I will find you someone excellent to continue with."

Nick, of course, laughed at the "unrelenting irony."

We continued to argue, banter and make up our own words. *Stomple* was always my favorite, one I had thought up in anger while trying to suggest that he stomped and trampled me when I was trying to speak. *Stomple* came out instead.

We, all of sudden, were written up in a Vancouver gossip column after he landed a leading role on a top TV series. In a trendy café, he was expressing loudly that he wouldn't be yelling if he didn't care. When I tried to go to the ladies' room, he said, "Not till we are done." He then told me all that was wrong with me and that I couldn't go outside for a smoke.

"I imagine this is what EST would have been like in the seventies—you can't leave the room, even to pee; you're in nicotine withdrawal while you are told that you are an asshole in front of a room full of people, all of whom have their eyes on you." I nodded in different directions to show him that the entire room was staring at him "caring for me." The write-up provided good PR for his new role.

Back in LA, when the show was in summer reruns, he gave me a sculptural silver pendant handcrafted by a local artisan. Representing female empowerment, it was set with an amethyst for enlightenment.

That night we were out at a party, and it clicked just as someone was snapping a Polaroid of Nick, his friend Philippe and me. I was starting to really get fed up with our platonic relationship. As the photo was developing in my hand, the entire year came into focus. Nick was looking at Philippe in the way I had always wished he'd look at me. The clearer the Polaroid became, the more I saw what I had missed. There was an entire story unfolding within the glances and body language that the picture revealed. I was somehow standing there between them, but they were together.

I waited until we were driving home on the freeway and asked nonchalantly, "Have you ever had a bisexual experience?" He pulled over to the shoulder.

Clearing his throat, he admitted to having one bisexual experience during the twelfth grade. Then he confessed that the more serious relationships were always with women, but around the time he met me, he had also met Philippe, and he began to deal with and feel what he had suppressed for most of his life. Three things went through my mind: We were at a complete standstill on the freeway, and since the plane hadn't crashed at LAX, the odds were I would get killed in a car. More important, at the exact same time I was falling in love with him, he was falling for a man. The pieces of jewelry he bought made more sense for him than me. As symbolized by the pendants he had given me, he was trying to find his feminine side fearlessly and had been enlightened. And he went pinging off like the bracelet in a different direction.

Once safely in his house, I thought how this was the first time I'd started seeing a therapist regularly. While I was having weekly sessions, I had chosen the most unavailable man I could possibly find—the one my therapist deemed my most healthy relationship to date. When I got home to New York and told her this, it would be our final session together, after which she would be dumping me for another life. This still wasn't the end of the story.

I was in LA for two more days. The final one was to celebrate Nick's birthday and to not be alone on the second anniversary of the day my mother died.

We talked a lot for the next few days and after that. He had felt terrible for not being able to tell me, but he was just figuring it all out himself and he had told no one, scared of what it could do to his career. I knew Nick loved and cared for me, had taught me so much and truly accepted everything about me. I wanted to do the same for Nick and did my best to come to terms with the fact that he was having the relationship with Philippe I wanted with him. I started to figure out my feelings and work on building a more stable friendship. Then I went out and found a new therapist.

CHAPTER 11

Cartier Tank Watch

I DON'T REMEMBER GETTING dressed for this funeral, except for fastening his classic 18K gold Cartier Tank with the black leather crocodile band around my wrist, looking down at it and being reminded of how it suited him: the width, the size, the simple black Roman numerals. It had an almost-aloof sense of style, much like the man who wore it.

I remember hailing the cab, with my coat tossed over my arm in the middle of winter. I hadn't thought to put it on until I arrived at the synagogue on Seventy-sixth Street and Amsterdam, shivering, my nose and feet numb. When my brothers called to ask if I needed a ride, I had thanked them, told them I wanted to be alone until I had to be there. I remember friends standing outside while I lit a cigarette and thought about the first time he left.

I had watched him drive away in his burgundy convertible Eldorado from our living room picture window and tried to will him back. I wanted it to be the way it was two days earlier, before my parents had announced they were getting a divorce. I wanted to be twelve, without the responsibility of explaining to my younger brothers, without having to comfort my mother, without grown-up talk about his affairs and the woman he was leaving us for. I wanted the father who danced with my mother to their song, Bobby Rydell's spunky version of "More." I wanted the father who pretended to be a radio announcer on car trips to keep my brothers amused, who took us to Shea Stadium when the Jets still played there and, while I was frozen and bored, bought me hot dogs and tried to get me to understand an incomplete pass.

My father and I listened to music together. One minute he was putting Henry Mancini on our record player; the next minute he surprised me by placing the needle down on the first Monkees album, which I wanted so badly and which he'd bought me on his way home from work. I loved when he'd arrive home, just around the time *This Is Tom Jones* was on television, rip off his tie along with Tom and sing "It's Not Unusual," trying to pop and sway his hips, his unguarded goofiness charming both my mother and me. But that was before the divorce. I am not sure what changed. When he left our house, he promised he would always be my father. But I never expected the new indifference he felt toward me and disappointment in me: the way I looked, my grades in school and my choices in college, men, life; that I'd never be pretty enough or smart enough or perfect enough to be the daughter he sang to sleep every night to the song "Daddy's Little Girl" when I was an infant and who he danced the twist with when I was a preteen. I'd never again be the daughter who felt safe in his arms when he scooped me up and rushed to the emergency room when I went into anaphylactic shock from a bee sting or whose hospital bed he sat at when I had my appendix out at six years old.

After two of my best friends each lost their dad while I was in high school, I called him and said, "Look, you are my father. I might not respect some of the things you've done and how you treated Mom. I hate that you pick at my weight, telling me I am too fat or too thin, tell me I need eyeliner, tell me I will never make a living as a writer and to choose another career instead. I hate that you don't hug anymore and that you are so tough on Eric and David, but I love you, and we are going to have a relationship!"

To which he said, "Yes; okay. I wish you would respect me, but thank you for never judging me." He never said *I love you*. He tightened up whenever I or anyone else went to give him a hug; he picked on my looks and my career choices well into my adulthood. We had honest talks about his adultery, when I would try to get him to be faithful to my stepmother throughout their twenty years together. It never worked. He finally left her for his third wife.

We shared an eye for style and an affinity for fashion. From the time I was young, I would help him choose different colors for the fabric patterns his company produced, and we talked texture and tones. He appreciated my clothing choices, yet I was probably the only kid in America besides my brothers who never bought her dad a tie on Father's Day. He had impeccable taste, and I was petrified to make the wrong decision. After purchasing my mom a watch instead of a ring for their engagement, he grew to love and collect timepieces and wore Vacheron Constantin and Audemars Piguet and other Swiss brands, but his streamlined Cartier Tank was his favorite. I remember how fine and elegant it looked on his wrist.

Right before my dad got sick, Tom Jones was playing at Manhattan's Webster Hall. I got tickets for us, thinking it would be fun to take him. I don't know why, after all these years, I'd wanted to do something special for him or why I knew it would make him happy. We went and we danced. Both Tom and my dad were older, but neither of them seemed to notice or care. My father sang "Delilah" as we walked down the street after the concert, and we laughed; I felt closer to him than I had in years. A month later he was diagnosed with a malignant tumor in his left kidney. It was the first time I'd ever seen my father in a hospital bed. It was the first time I'd ever seen him with more than a cold or sinus trouble. I was allowed to give him ice to suck on. The doctor came in and told me they would have the tests back soon, but they thought they had gotten all the cancer. My father was weak and fragile, and for the first time since the day he rushed me to the emergency room, he looked vulnerable. He called me over and said, "I don't want anyone else to see me like this." He blushed as he asked me to bring the bedpan and to draw the curtains. He was sixty-four and I was thirty-eight. A month after the kidney came out, they told us the cancer had spread to his bones. It was only five and a half years since my mom had died, when he rested his hand on my back at the funeral home when we said our good-byes and he put his arm around me at her burial plot.

I remember walking into the side door at his service to get to our seats next to my uncle, my father's brother, and I remember reaching out to grab onto my own brothers as they had grabbed onto me at our mom's funeral, where I held up the two of them, both six foot three and built like football players. But when my hands went for theirs, I grasped air. They had wives and children of their own now, and I felt completely and utterly alone. I had to pull it together and say something I had written the night before in honor of my father's memory. The rabbi asked me to talk about the man who gave me mixed signals and messages throughout my life. I relied on humor; I relied on memories of our both being lefties and his teaching me how to play first base. He always thought I needed more makeup. Even at ninety-eight pounds, with pain patches and barely able to eat, he asked, "Where are your blush and your lipstick?" He seemed to be channeling my grandmother. I teased him about getting back together when he saw my mother again "up there," when we knew it wouldn't be much longer, when the chemo wasn't working and he had decided to stop the treatment. We laughed about my continuous attempts to try to get them back together, even after they were both remarried. He joked back, saying, "Okay, I'll give it another go, if she'll have me." And then he rubbed my palm and confessed she was the only woman he'd truly loved. "We just weren't right together. I wasn't right for anyone, and it was no one's problem but my own." He continued weakly. "I couldn't get truly close to any woman. The more your mom tried to save our relationship, the more I backed away. Until she had finally had enough, and then I didn't want to leave."

"I remember," I said, trying to shake off the feeling of my throat closing up, the memories, vivid as if they had happened only recently instead of twenty-five years before.

I'd been in therapy long enough to process all of this, just not long enough to stop reliving it and fearing loss through my own romantic relationships. I wasn't only trying to keep my parents together; I was also trying to work out my earlier feelings that my father had left me, by staying too long with emotionally unavailable men who could not give me what I needed. And now I was losing my father all over again, for good.

He only wanted me and his third wife to take care of him. He had been married to her for only a year. I stayed over when she was away on business. I spent sleepless hours making sure he wouldn't stop breathing in the middle of the night. He left boxes for me to look through, stories in literary journals I wrote that I thought he'd never read, photos of my mom and him, of my brothers as captains of their football teams at various high school games.

Although he was frail, he still liked to wear a watch, and the Cartier Tank was the most comfortable. He would put his newly acquired glasses on to check the time. "How much time left?" He asked the doctor to give it to him straight at one of the last appointments I took him to.

"A month at the most." And then the doctor told me I might want to start to setting up hospice. I thought about how his body was shutting down, just as he was opening up to me.

"Do you still have your mom's watch?" he asked. I said yes, rolled my eyes and said I wanted a ring if I ever got engaged. I told him that I now wore only vintage men's timepieces because of how much their story had confused me. But I still wore my mom's diamond art deco watch on special occasions.

I had his sarcasm, he said. I liked to think of it as irony or dry and subtle wit.

"I've always been so proud of your independence and your heart. I should have told you all these years how beautiful you are. I am sorry I never knew how." He took the Cartier Tank off and strapped it around my wrist; I helped him with the clasp. A week later he went into a coma and was gone.

Unlike the memories of my mother's funeral, I can't recall whether I wore a dress or pants or the shoes I chose. I remember putting on blush, lipstick and eyeliner and fastening his watch tightly, thankful for the moments I'd spent learning who he was again, and knowing that this time, although he would always be with me, I really did have to say good-bye.

CHAPTER 12

Princess Sparkle

I BOLTED OFF A plane, holding huge pink Disney "Princess" shopping bags in each hand, looking around eagerly to see her. I felt a tug at my sweater. I bent down. "Hi," she said. Her blue eyes gleamed and her lips turned up into a mischievous smile as she draped her arms around my neck. "Big hug," she told me. I could feel how much she had grown in the four months since I'd last seen her. Her blond hair had gotten blonder, cascading down to the middle of her back. Her legs were longer, all traces of baby fat gone. She was dressed in a white tank top and capris, a lavender-colored cardigan with a metallic flower pendant around her neck and a charm bracelet, a solitaire ring, a handbag and pearl dangles. "Get your stuff," she insisted, leading me toward the baggage claim, "so we can get home and play." I noticed a wiggle in her walk. She would break hearts one day.

Watching her, I remembered why I left New York at five thirty a.m., got on a plane and endured nearly two hours of turbulence. I am Sammie's aunt.

She offered me her French fries, asked if they were still my favorite. "Uh-huh," I said, shoving them into my mouth.

"It's so funny," she said. "Don't you think?"

"What?" I asked, already amused at how she expressed herself at six years old.

"You know, that we've always liked the same things." She slipped her hand into mine, and we connected again as though we had never been apart, and as though the seven hundred some-odd miles between New York and Indianapolis didn't exist. My brother tapped me on the shoulder and said, "Hey, remember me?"

Every visit, Sammie gets a little taller, a little bossier and a little more independent—a little more like me. And back then, it got harder for me to leave. When I was with her, I could pretend I wasn't forty-two, single and alone. I had someone with whom to talk, laugh, share confidences, play dress up and shop for jewelry and clothes—a special person to love.

As a long-distance aunt, I was constantly rearranging my time—planning my free weekends, vacations and holidays around seeing her—to ensure continuity and in the beginning, to reassure myself she wouldn't forget me. Still, I missed crucial moments: her first steps, the first time the tooth fairy came and the magic of her dressing up for Halloween. But, somehow, despite the time and distance between us, our relationship has grown stronger.

I was thirty-five when I learned I was going to be an aunt for the first time. Since the title didn't come with a job description and there was no *What to Expect When You're Expecting a Niece*, I had no idea of the mixed emotions I would feel when my baby brother called me at four a.m. to tell me he had a baby girl. Excitedly, I asked questions: Her name? "Samantha Taylor." Weight? "Six pounds, eight ounces." Hair? "Sort of." Who does she look like? "Grandpa Willie when he was ninety." After I hung up the phone, the laughter and pride caught in my throat and I was overcome by the sibling rivalry my brother and I had engaged in growing up. *It's not fair. I'm the older sister; I should be having a child first.* The news that should have filled me with complete joy filled me with self-pity, doubt and the fear that perhaps my biological clock had been on snooze.

The next day, all traces of envy were gone. I had a niece. A girl. I got busy making her a jewelry box. The basic design of natural wood with hooks and drawers and ring holders was already done by a friend. I painted it antique rose, and then I gold leafed and decoupaged it with all things feminine: cupids, stars, moons, hearts, flowers, cherubs, all styles of jewelry and little swirls of ribbon with sayings. By the time I got past the glue and spray paint to the shellac, I realized that my apartment was not adequately ventilated and nearly passed out from all the fumes. But it had the desired effect. Later on when Sammie was two, she told me, "It was more beautiful than anything in the world." She'd spill out the contents and we'd go through them, as she showed me which was her "real" and "play" jewelry.

Once the box was finished, the next few months were spent giggling my way into debt at Baby Gap and ducking into Barnes & Noble for *Charlotte's Web* and *Little Women* for when she was older. I then bought the more useful gifts: a 14K gold miniature heart locket, into which I slipped a small photo of my mom, a pair of floral rose gold studs for when she got her ears pierced and a baby ID bracelet with an engravable plaque and freshwater pearls. "You can't give her any of these things yet," my sister-in-law cautioned. "She'll choke on them."

"Really?" I said, feigning shock. At thirty-six, I was aware of what infants could and could not teethe on. I wanted to be the first person to purchase her jewelry that she would cherish and remember later on, and that would connect us as it had my grandmother, mom and me.

I'd be lying if I said it was love at first sight for Sammie and me. When I lifted her into my arms, she wailed and flailed like a miniature version of Linda Blair in *The Exorcist* and spit up three times on my favorite cashmere sweater. "Is she supposed to cry this much?" I asked my sister-in-law.

"She hasn't stopped since we brought her home."

It was easily another ninety minutes of dancing her around the room, singing every show tune I could think of, until my sister-in-law asked if either one of us was ever going to quiet down.

As Sammie's eyes began to close, I slid onto the couch, her soft baby head nestled in the crease of my neck. Both of us were exhausted and conked out. She woke me up by grabbing my antique diamond solitaire necklace in her tiny hands, looked at me quizzically and then broke into a big toothless, drooly smile. And that was when I knew she was part of me.

Mommy would be the one to deal with tantrums, change diapers and teach her that pens don't belong in electrical outlets. Mommy would worry when she had a fever, tell her she was brave and wipe her tears every time she went to the doctor to get a shot.

I would be the person who would teach her to create a tiara by gluing shimmery sequins and sparkles. I'd show her how to draw hearts and flowers in different Crayola shades of her favorite color, pink. I'd let her pull out all my jewelry and dress her in the pieces that would make her look like her favorite Disney princess. I'd let her eat too many French fries, blow on her pizza to cool it and heat it up when she said she wanted spaghetti instead. I'd sneak Coca-Cola into her sippy cup, let her stay up way past bedtime and watch *Beauty and the Beast* with her five times in a row.

I'd never be too tired to detangle necklaces, never too busy to talk, never too cynical to be swept away by her innocence and turned back into a kid again myself. That is the part of being an aunt that no one tells you about: that you get to have your childhood back; that you get to eat little half-baked cakes made in Easy Bake Ovens, see how long you can keep the hula hoop spinning, play dress up and pretend that cascades of metallic Mardi Gras beads are royal sashes, that the possibility of losing your job won't matter when you're Cinderella at the ball.

Ever since Sammie turned two, she has explored her individuality through jewelry. Blond with aqua-blue eyes, she switched which Disney princess she wanted to be each week, trying out her personal style. She was Belle, the Southern beauty with the bib necklace, the regal Aurora with the dazzling gemstone pendant, Jasmine with the exotic jewels and Cinderella, who went from rags to riches and basically piled on everything, a look that Sammie came to adore.

Like most young girls between the ages of two and five, she had a passion for pink. Daywear included bubble-gum-hued lamé dresses with full ballerina skirts, sparkly handbags and, most important, an armful of bangles and ropes of crystal beads. We'd spend hours in the Disney Store, surrounded by all things glittery. There were crowns and glass slippers and the enchantment of castles and moats. Sammie got the hang of saying, "I have to have that," pointing and stamping her foot while grabbing onto a large cocktail ring that could have fit around her wrist. Yet she could be mesmerized out of a tantrum by the swinging of a long diamanté pendant.

Sammie's known my phone number since she was three.

She can recount the highlights of every visit. Everything I taught her, everything she taught me, has stuck. A bond formed out of shimmery nail polish, sequins, Play-Doh and Elmer's Glue. Although Sammie grew out of dressing for school in ornately accessorized nightgowns, she never outgrew me. Little custom-made birthday cards with sticky twinkly gemstones began to arrive each year, and holding my hand became more an expression of affection than a necessity.

By the time she was six she'd gotten her ears pierced, and we'd pile baskets full of trendy, inexpensive, costume jewelry up at Claire's. She'd hold up dangly earrings to her ears, pile power bead bracelets up her arm to her elbow and layer necklaces down her tiny chest. We had switched to watching *What a Girl Wants* instead of *Little Mermaid*, and she was asking, "Do I look like Amanda Bynes?" instead of trying to emulate Ariel.

As for me, I had gone through all the developmental stages of being a single aunt. I learned how to playact. When shoppers stopped me at the supermarket to tell me what a beautiful child I had, how she had my eyes, I'd beam and thank them, feeling no guilt for pretending she was mine.

On her seventh birthday, she wanted a jewelry party. I was called in to help ten girls create bracelets crafted out of stretchy wire and all different kinds of beads including Murano glass, various colored crystals, silver initials and animal, floral, heart, moon and star motifs. "My favorite color is green now, but I like it mixed up with a bit of purple and blue, and I don't want it too girly or matchy-matchy. I want it more bohemian," she explained.

"Where did you learn these words?" I asked.

"From you, of course," she said. It was one of the highlights of the evening. The other was when many of her friends got the bracelets they "dreamt of" and told Sammie, "Your aunt is the coolest person I know."

In earlier years, I talked nonstop about Sammie to everyone who would listen. Some of my more polite friends asked me to stop boring them to death. Others looked at me as if I were a lunatic, except for Jodi, my oldest friend, whose niece Lindsay is the exact same age as Sammie. When Sammie was two, I told Jodi, "It's so cute. She starts every conversation with either 'Guess what?' or 'Can I tell you something?' "

"Sammie has conversations?" Jodi asked suspiciously.

"What, Lindsay doesn't?"

They are the children of our younger siblings. They were the reason we felt the sudden and overwhelming urge to work less and go out and find husbands fast; why we had forsaken buying fall shoes to go shopping at the Disney Store and why we started talking dream playhouses instead of sex.

"Don't worry," I told Jodi. "Lindsay is so cute. Some kids just start talking more quickly, and Lindsay is good at putting foreign objects in her mouth."

"Does Sammie do that?"

"No, of course not. She is way too smart."

These conversations reached the level of competition, such as who learned to spell, write and get the hang of the potty first. "Do you realize we are acting like two mothers comparing their kids on the playground?"

"We're acting out," Jodi said one day, before asking, "Do you think we will ever have kids of our own?"

Six years later, the question still hung like a comic strip blurb over my head.

On the last day of my visit, Sammie and I played dress-up Barbies on a computer game. She taught me the program on the family PC. We changed the color of everything from their hair and eyes to the shoes and styled them in different clothes and jewelry. "Oh no, change that," Sammie said after giving the redhead the rubies. "She will look much better with sapphires." She touched my necklace, which she had once grabbed onto when she was an infant and said, "I only want real diamonds, not anything fake."

"How can you tell?" I asked, suspecting she was parroting my sister-in-law.

"Because that's what you wear," she said.

"We have time to watch one movie before you leave." She picked out *Sleeping Beauty* for old times' sake.

"You're not watching," she said, her inquisitive face pressed against mine.

"Am too," I told her.

"Are not." She pried open my eyes with her fingers. "And you're going to miss the prince."

"I am Sleeping Beauty and I'm waiting for the prince to kiss me and wake me up," I said, hoping this would allow me to nap for five minutes.

"Don't be silly. You know the prince isn't real and the story is only make-believe."

I do? Maybe I should stop wondering when he's going to show up.

"Okay. I'm waiting for my husband, then."

"You can't have a husband. If you did, you wouldn't have enough time to play with me."

CHAPTER 13

The Brooch

I
T WAS GETTING close to Mother's Day when I got home from Indiana, and I was already missing my niece, and now my mom, like hell. I engaged in a few hours of self-pity, most of which were spent lying on the couch, entrenched in thoughts of how I might have missed out on having my own daughter and the questions of whether it was too late or if I ever would. I remembered telling my mom that if I ever had kids, I'd want her to be in the delivery room with me. "I couldn't imagine what going through nine months of your being pregnant would be like, with your calling me to describe every ache, pain and feeling of bloat and indigestion," she teased. "The thought of going through labor with you is even more scary."

My grandmother joined in. "Within five minutes you'd be begging Beth to 'forget natural childbirth' and get the doctor to give her the epidural before it was too late." They both laughed at my expense.

"Do you think you could be overlooking the possibility that my hypochondriacal tendencies could have been formed, say, when you didn't let anyone touch me as an infant until they washed their hands, when you thought I'd get a disease akin to leprosy after having my ears pierced or the bubonic plague from the sandbox?" I asked my mom.

I began to contemplate the women on the maternal side of my family and how we've all reinvented and redefined ourselves at various moments, to assert our independence, overcome grief or change our lives.

I picked up the tarnished antique sterling silver frame that I've kept on my nightstand since coming home from college and looked closely at the four women in the faded photograph. I noticed our differences, marked mostly by our ages and hairstyles. I am thirteen, gangly with braces and a blow-dried straight mane parted down the middle. My mom, Shirley, is thirty-five. Her light brown locks are shoulder length, wild and curly. Nana Ida, fifty-six, is bottle blond and perfectly coiffed. My great-grandmother Fanny's cherub face is framed by chin-length bobbed hair. She is seventy-nine in the picture, taken in 1973.

At a closer glance, I also see our similarities, the traits that have been passed down through four generations of the maternal side of my family. Humongous feet and even larger ears, a propensity for worrying and the fine art of guilt by manipulation immediately come to mind.

I learned independence and strength, and that irony and humor help you get through the roughest of times. I come from a sentimental lot of women who kept every card and letter they ever received. (I know this because I also inherited all of their keepsake boxes.) The female mantra repeated to me since I was younger was "Never go out of the house, even to the corner, without looking your best. You never know who you're going to meet."

To this, my grandmother added, "Never without a little lipstick and earrings to brighten your face and a smile to brighten up someone else's day."

While our essential character and some of our physical traits were similar, our personal styles and our interpretations of looking our best were undeniably different, especially when it came to our taste in jewelry. Nana Fanny was an understated woman who wore only three pieces of jewelry: a simple Russian rose gold wedding band outlined with an etched scroll pattern, small drop rose gold and European cut diamond earrings, and an Edwardian brooch with a center opal surrounded by a garland motif of small diamonds from which dropped a larger bezel-set old mine cut diamond*. It was a sizable pin but

---

* Old mine cut diamonds, which have a cushion shape on the edges, became predominant in nineteenth-century jewelry. They were the predecessor to the brilliant cut. However, these diamonds are cut with a higher crown (top) and a deeper pavilion (base) and wider culet (facet at

still elegant and feminine. She came over from Russia to the United States when she was nineteen, after marrying my great-grandfather Papa David, and had three children: Nana Ida, the eldest; Sam, the middle child; and Sylvia, the youngest. My great-grandparents fled during wartime and, like most Russian immigrants, they left without most of the family jewelry. They either sold whatever pieces they had to help them pay for transport or left heirlooms with relatives, too scared that precious gems would be confiscated from them. Nana Fanny came with only her wedding band on her finger and earrings in her ears; the diamonds were taken out and brought to the United States much later on by a distant cousin. But for their twenty-fifth wedding anniversary, Papa David, who owned a small coat factory, wanted to do something special. I remember Nana Ida telling my mom and me that Papa David had a friend in the jewelry business who needed coats for his three daughters, his sister and his wife. He did a trade with him for the pin, which turned out to be a rare opal in platinum from the Edwardian era.

Unlike many of my friends who had lost one or both of

---

the very bottom). They do not have as much fire as the modern-day brilliant cut. They do have character in their age, shape and imperfect beauty and sometimes a larger appearance because of how they are fashioned. They have made a major comeback in the past ten to fifteen years, and the new versions are referred to as cushion cuts. They have been perfected by today's stone cutters and are an extremely popular choice for engagement rings and earrings in white and natural-colored diamonds.

their grandmothers, I felt privileged to know both my maternal and paternal ones and spend time with my great-grandmother until I was fourteen. I heard much of Fanny's story from Nana Ida. My great-grandmother was a discreet woman who was self-conscious about her Russian accent. She loved hearing about my school, friends and camp. She would wear her brooch on dresses that she sewed herself: different versions of short-sleeved, nipped-waist, full-skirted, calf-length styles in pale colors and neutrals, in wool gabardines in the winter and lightweight cotton piques in the summer. She would wear the brooch to cook family dinners, to visit with friends on the bench outside her apartment building in the Bronx and to holidays at Nana Ida's house in Brooklyn.

My early memories of Nana Fanny were of her hair before she grew older and cut it into the shorter bob style. Earlier on it was almost all white, down to her waist and she wore it twisted in a bun. I'd climb into her lap and ask her to take it down. We'd play beauty parlor; she'd teach me how to make braids and how to use decorative Bakelite combs. "One day my hair will be as long as yours and I will be as beautiful as you," I'd say, and her cheeks would turn all rosy. She beamed when Nana Ida, my mom and I were around. She never said too much in English, but she would talk to Nana Ida in part Yiddish, part Russian, always with laughing eyes that hid a life of raising three kids on very little money in a two-bedroom apartment in East New York.

She wore the brooch like a badge of strength and would take it off only for me. I was fascinated by the changing color of the opal and the little fiery flecks. She was a proud woman. "Always dress like company is coming," she'd say as she fastened the pin to my shirts or sweaters.

Nana Ida preferred making an entrance. She wore huge cocktail rings that covered up half her fingers and large button or clip earrings. She loved color, particularly turquoise, jade and deep red coral. She also liked big beads and pearls that she wore in short strands around her neck. She had her "good pieces," art deco styles that she purchased with savvy from pawnshops, which were where, she had learned, antiques dealers went to find their most coveted pieces, before there were auctions, markets and shows. Nana Ida got the measles when she was a child. "I lost most of the hearing in my left ear and had to have my head shaved. For one year until my hair grew back, I was made fun of at school and I always had it in my mind that I would be the belle of the ball when I was older," she told me one night while we were playing dress up. She taught herself to Charleston and then to waltz and speak without any hint of an East New York or Brooklyn accent. Nana Fanny sewed all Ida's dresses to wear to dances, where she had many suitors but chose Papa Rubin, my grandfather, for his heart, which he gave totally and completely to her and his family. She became the matriarch of his large six-sibling clan of five brothers and one sister. Papa Rubin worked for a printing company and Nana Ida worked for a large hat store until my mom was born. She knew how to save and she knew how to bargain. She found peplum waist suits and sleek shirtdresses at Gimbels and Bonwit Teller sales and she scoured the secondhand jewelry and pawnshops, where she found her cuff bracelets made out of Bakelite or carved wood, cocktail rings and the fine art deco jewels that she combined with costume and crystal beads. While never ostentatious, her big heart was only outsized by her bold, statement pieces. She liked being noticed. She had artsy friends who were painters and writers. She drank in culture, listened carefully and went to the library to understand all that was around her. She figured out how to make simple food and leftovers interesting. "I had a way with chicken. I could turn one large bird into a week's worth of different dishes. I also learned a trick or two with rice and noodles." Her creativity with staples as well as finances allowed her to save to travel to Italy, France, Israel, Spain and South America, collecting friends, experiences and souvenirs of various styles of jewelry along the way.

Around the time of the photo, my mother had gone totally natural, this time trading in her Jane Fonda *Klute* shag for a Carole King circa *Tapestry* frizz fest. She had stopped wearing my clothes and wore her own tie-dyed jean outfits, peasant shirts and flowing maxiskirts with magnifying glass pendants, chokers on velvet ribbons and sterling silver rings, outlined in filigree. When she went back to work in the fashion business in the later seventies, rising through the ranks to vice president, she traded in her embroidered Faded Glory denim, slouchy handbags, long necklaces and Zuni turquoise for Donna Karan matte jersey and for the more innovative artisan and sculptural jewelry of Robert Lee Morris, Patricia von Muslin and Elsa Peretti. Eventually, she began collecting and wearing period jewelry: cut steel bracelets and onyx lockets of the early nineteenth century, which went well with her black, no-fuss, no-frills wardrobe.

I remember my grandmother's strong opinions on the way my mom dressed. "Shirley, please don't try and tell me that suit is 'midnight navy' and not black. Is there a difference? It's still dark and brings you down. What's wrong with adding a few pastels to your wardrobe?"

Each generation passed down advice to the next. "Ida, try a little pink and less coral in your lipstick," Fanny once said.

"If you go to do your laundry in your overalls and your hair up in a 'Pebbles' ponytail, you might never meet someone," my mom would tell me.

When I was sixteen, two years after Nana Fanny passed away, I noticed that Ida was wearing the large oval opal from the brooch on her finger surrounded by an outline of diamonds.

"How could you change your mother's pin, something that's so sentimental?" I asked her.

"Jewelry is meant to be worn and treasured. Grandma Fanny would have wanted me to wear it rather than just let it sit in a jewelry box," she responded. "By wearing the opal,

I feel my mother's presence and she's always with me." It made sense. To her, the jewelry became more special, even though it wasn't in its original setting. She had the mine cut diamond made into a clasp for a strand of pearls.

When she and my grandfather retired to Florida and her lifestyle changed, my grandmother gave all her "important" jewelry to my mom.

My mother went to the same jeweler who revamped the pieces the first time and had the five carat opal cut down to a more wearable three-carat ring, accented by a creative bezel-set pattern. She had the mine cut diamond turned into a stickpin. With each transformation, the original brooch was taking on the personal style of each wearer.

When my mom passed away and I finally opened her jewelry box, I headed back to the same shop where my mother had gone and where the son had taken over the family business. I had him turn the opal into a pendant with a fine floral and leaf motif surrounding it, similar to the design of the original brooch, although much more dainty. The diamond stickpin was made into a shorter pendant so I could layer them.

When Mother's Day finally arrived, I lay on the couch, watching a double feature of *Terms of Endearment* and *One True Thing*, thinking of eating Mallomars in honor of her. I figured this would allow me to have one great big cry, get it all out and go on the next day.

But then I spoke to my grandmother, who, from Florida,

seemed to sense what I was doing and said, "Get off your couch. It's time to get a little air. Remember to put on a little lipstick and a smile and please change out of your pajamas before you hit the street. A pair of jeans and a sweater might be more apropos to walking around your neighborhood. You never know—"

"'Who you are going to meet,'" I chimed in.

I then remembered my special visit with Sammie, whom I can share these photos with, who loves jewelry almost as much as I do, and who, while we braid each other's hair, asks me to tell her stories about my mom, her grandmother. She has humongous feet and big ears. She definitely knows how to manipulate. She remembers when she was five and I gave her advice: "You look just like a princess in that pink nightgown, but maybe for school you should change and wear the denim skirt."

When she turned ten, she started asking, "So, when are you going to give me the necklaces?"

"When you are twenty-one," I told her, and realized I chose an arbitrary age just as when my mom told me I could get my ears pierced.

"How about for my sweet sixteen?" She rested her head on my shoulder. I struck a deal and told her I would give her the diamond necklace when she was sixteen and the opal . . . someday. She was cool with that.

The next time we both visited with Nana Ida, her great-grandmother, who was ninety-two at the time, Sammie sat

on her lap and Nana Ida told her, "The necklaces Beth had made are too small. I need a microscope to see them."

Sammie teased her back. "I think they will make a great pair of mismatched earrings." I looked at the two of them, happy to still have two generations on the maternal side of my family with whom I could share these moments. The jewelry would never lose its sentimental value no matter what form it took. The real keepsake was that it would allow me to remember where I came from and keep the women who inspired me close to my heart.

"It represents that we are all part of one another and always will be," Sammie said.

CHAPTER 14

Self-Purchase

A FTER RECEIVING THE heirlooms passed down from my mother and the watch from my father, reworking Nana Fanny's brooch, designing my own collection and launching my consulting firm, I found that my appreciation for jewelry deepened and led me back to my roots to include writing for magazines once again. Right after I had turned forty-one, I was recommended by a longtime colleague, with whom I had worked on one of the fashion publications, for a position as editor-at-large on a contract basis for an established national jewelry trade magazine. This allowed me the opportunity to continue my own businesses and freelance articles for women's magazines, while writing about jewelry on a regular basis.

I was completely entrenched in the history, culture, lore and legend of this art form, and I took a position as sales

manager on Fridays and Saturdays for a well-known antique jewelry guru who has a treasure chest of a store on Madison Avenue. We had met at an event, and she approached me afterward, complimenting me on my style and confiding that I reminded her of herself, thirty-five years earlier, when she opened the shop. I was mesmerized by the background behind the museum-quality jewels as well as by her gift for storytelling. Age seventy-four, she had an ex-husband with whom she was still friends and a son and grandchild she adored. She'd found her soul mate in her fifties and traveled the globe, soaking in the colors of India, scouring the vast flea markets of London and Paris and falling in love with jewelry she bought, traded and bargained for. I worked for her to learn hands-on the history of jewelry, and to wear on my own hands, wrists and fingers the fabulous period pieces that ranged from the eighteenth through early twentieth centuries. With each tidbit she revealed about gems, she also slipped in an anecdote that would relate to my dating habits and my life as a single woman in New York. On one occasion when I was dating a guy she did not trust, she took out her 10X jeweler's loupe and taught me how to see through it and tell the difference between what was real and what could easily be mistaken as authentic.

I got to meet other dealers and learned the ins and outs of how to buy all types of jewelry, and I wrote how-to articles on the subject for consumer and lifestyle magazines.

I began spending most weekends ogling expensive bau-

bles in fine shops throughout Manhattan, from established houses such as Cartier and Van Cleef & Arpels to the majestic and magical windows of Fred Leighton. Although my penchant for period pieces grew to include art nouveau, art deco and retro in addition to Georgian and Edwardian/belle époque, I became an equal-opportunity jewelry fan. I visited Barneys, Bergdorf and the Fragments store as well as artisan shops in Manhattan, where I could easily be seduced by contemporary designer styles and where fancy natural-colored diamonds caused my heart to flutter.

One Saturday, while leaning over a display case to take a closer look at a pair of small diamond cushion cut drop earrings in a Fifth Avenue shop, I sensed a presence beside me. A deep voice inquired, "Could you try this on for me?" A steady hand held out an elegant antique engagement ring. I glanced at the ring and then looked up into the most intense green eyes, dark wavy hair and a slightly shy smile. The guy was gorgeous; how could I say no?

I tried on a total of ten rings for him, from intricate turn-of-the-century styles to clean modern settings. He placed a deposit on my favorite and thanked me.

Having had my fair share of catastrophes with men buying me jewelry, I was glad to help. I congratulated him and resisted the urge to say, *Here's my card in case it doesn't work out.*

Later that day, I thought back to some of my earlier mishaps, which ranged from *What the hell was he thinking?* to the more sentimental gifts bestowed on me, such as finding out

the guys I was seeing were dating, getting engaged or were already married to someone else. For much of my life, I'd been either a serial monogamist or in between boyfriends. I'd also been given jewelry that ranged from silver artisan sculptures to silver-skull-and-crossbones-on-heavy-leather-cord designs to sweet, girly diamond-accented hearts of all sizes. These guys were buying for how they envisioned me, rather than for who I actually was. I had earrings that weighed as heavy on my lobes as ill-fated romances on my heart. There were whimsical charms, which were fun in the beginning, but, like the rest of these pieces, had about the same endurance as the relationships they represented.

Some of my all-time doozies included Jay, who, prior to dating someone else while he was still dating me, told me he very much believed in exchanging gifts on Valentine's Day. I understood that he was a writer barely scraping by at the time, so I was fine with the regifting of a ring he had held on to from college. But after opening the small box with the reused ribbon, I had my first sign the relationship would not last, not because I realized he had given me a band his college girlfriend had given to him and that he had forgotten he had once shown me, but because it was almost the exact same inlaid-turquoise-style ring that was offered and taken back by Victor in the fifth grade. Not only was I choosing similar men, but they also were giving me the same kind of jewelry.

Speaking of this gemstone, not long after Jay and before

Liam, I dated a guy briefly, who said that my eyes were the color of turquoise and that he could see "forever" in them. Forever came a week later, when I found out he was seeing a woman he worked with and whose eyes were the same hue as, well, smoky topaz.

When I turned forty, I began to date a gorgeous, "legally separated" actor who, after a couple of months told me, "I don't really get the point of diamonds." We were curled up on my couch watching a DVD, and he was fiddling with one of my double drop diamond antique earrings. "They are colorless and lack character." I took a deep breath and paused the DVD.

"First of all, they aren't necessarily colorless," I explained patiently, pointing out celebrities who got beautiful pink and blue diamond engagement rings. He looked at me as if I were insane. I forgot that this was a guy obsessed with the Discovery Channel, and I tried a new tack. "They resist fire," I said.

Nothing. "And Marilyn Monroe sang about them."

He immediately perked up. "Yeah," he said dreamily. "In *Gentlemen Prefer Blondes*. But didn't they use fake stones in the film?"

Great, I thought. He knows all about CZ. My future flashed in front of me: coffeemakers, toaster ovens, gadgets and gizmos for the rest of my life—or worse, rhinestones and cubic zirconia instead of diamonds, rubies and emeralds. But as time went on, I thought I had the real thing. As for looks,

he was a mix of Richard Gere and Kurt Russell. He took my temperature and made homemade chicken soup when I had the flu, told me it was all right to vent after a bad day and put up with all of my neuroses. He cried with me at sad movies, without a hint of embarrassment, saying, "Man, that really did me in." Then I found out that he hadn't filed for a divorce, that she left because he had a gambling problem, and that he moved back in without telling me—all while his dog was still living at my house.

I got past thinking there was something wrong with me, not counting choosing extremely unavailable men. I took a hiatus from dating and started working more. Hunting for my own jewelry became as exhilarating as a new crush and much less dangerous to my heart.

I continued modeling jewelry for male friends and strangers, from long chandelier earrings to pearl necklaces. Since I write on the subject, many of my female friends deemed me an expert and sent their husbands to me for advice, pleading, "You've got to help me; he has such awful taste when it comes to choosing jewelry."

But does he kill spiders? I wanted to ask.

Eventually I got really tired of setting up my female and male friends with the perfect gem. I had yet to find the right one—a substantial and worthy jewel for myself.

I stopped wrestling with attraction verses affordability, desire versus debt, longing versus leftover mac and cheese from a box. Impulse and individual style won out. I finally

decided it was time to take the plunge from perusing to purchasing. It became clear that I needed to clear out all the pieces and relationships that no longer worked for me. I learned that it might be easier to find the right ring than the right man. I retired my trendy sterling silver, my cute white gold tiny diamond pendants and my small diamond studs, and I made a pact with myself to find a more important and dazzling piece of jewelry. I rationalized to make some trade-offs with my yearly budget: maneuver a two-day holiday when traveling on business instead of a five-day yearly vacation; take on more freelance work on weekends instead of going out with emotionally stunted men; take laundry to the house of my stepfather, brother or anyone who owned a washer and dryer instead of sending it out for seven bucks a pound; stick with one pair of boots and one pair of new sandals as a shoe budget for the year. Most important was to move around balances on credit cards to six-month promotional APRs.

My first self-purchase investment was a platinum eternity band with round diamonds set in a pattern of marquis and square shapes. Before long, I decided it needed a mate. Soon after, there was a family of seven thin geometric motifs from the 1920s through 1940s in platinum and with small diamonds, which I wear on my *right* index finger. I trade them off with a more organic stack in yellow and rose gold with more rough and unusual cut stones, floral motifs and vines and branches. The stacked look has become my signature.

Soon after I started wearing the first vintage mix, I was told by a Manhattan matchmaker I was writing about in an article that "you can't go out with a finger full of wedding and anniversary bands when you are trying to date. Men get confused. They don't remember which finger. They will think you are married or engaged. Or worse yet, they will think you have money to buy your own jewelry."

Sure enough, a guy came over to me in a restaurant, pointed to my finger and asked, "Is that how many times you've been married?"

"No," I shot back, "it's all the times I haven't."

He told me I was witty, handed me a napkin with his phone number and said to call him when I *didn't* want to get hitched again. As intriguing as it seemed, I wasn't in the market for another unavailable man when there were so many eligible pieces of jewelry to be found.

I became the proud owner of a wide platinum, ruby and diamond art deco bracelet; a pair of long, contemporary briolette cut diamond drop earrings; and a sexy 18K gold mesh choker with dangling multicolored sapphires.

Every time I bought another piece of jewelry for myself, my rationalizations went out the window. Even though as an editor and jewelry consultant I bought pieces at an insider's price, I still began feeling a twinge of guilt about my decadence and doubted I should be spending so elaborately on myself.

I never had any trouble buying a Gucci handbag or Prada

shoes. I had IRAs and mutual funds. Not only was I clad in designer clothes and starting a collection of jewelry, but I was responsibly or neurotically planning ahead for my retirement.

So why was I feeling so guilty? I remember my sweet sixteen. I had my eye on a sapphire pendant with tiny diamond accents. I brought my father to see it. "This is the kind of jewelry that your husband will buy for you," he said. He presented me with a sterling silver Elsa Peretti cuff from Tiffany & Co. instead. I loved it and still have it, but the message I heard was, "You're sterling until some man deems you gold or platinum."

Like many of my peers—single, divorced and married—I have grown out of the belief that jewelry, especially precious stones, must be purchased for a woman by a man. In much the same way, I've learned to turn down dates with men whom I am unsure about, build my own shelves and kill my own spiders. I'm self-reliant and independent. I've joined the growing ranks of self-purchasing women who are in touch with their tastes, more confident about their personal styles and know they've worked hard and are worth it.

For my forty-first birthday, I decided it was time for a more substantial necklace to replace my lone solitaire. I choose my jewelry stores carefully, selecting only those that offer welcoming and knowledgeable sales help, allow me to try on and to ask questions and never leave me waiting when they spot a woman with husband in tow, assuming a bigger purchase.

The necklace I picked was a delicate, lacy-garland style of varying-size diamonds with intricate milgrain work around each stone. Everywhere I go, women compliment me and ask for the name and address of the shop where I purchased it.

"I've been looking for a new pair of longer earrings. I'm thinking about pink diamonds," a coworker told me after seeing my necklace. "Why wait around for my husband to buy them?"

Whenever I put on my necklace, which has become my new favorite piece, I still get a lift. And if I ever do get married, I'm certain I will continue to buy my own jewelry (with the possible exception of the wedding ring). But it will be nice to hear someone say, "Honey, let me help you with the clasp."

CHAPTER 15

Cuff Links

"*B*ELISSIMO—THESE ARE ABSOLUTELY the most beautiful things I've ever seen," Paolo said, holding the cuff links up to the light. They were circular high cut onyx and diamond set in platinum. Although I'd had them custom made for him for his forty-third birthday and was hoping he would love them, I put my hand on my hip and scrunched my face, like a twelve-year-old in need of attention. "Oh, except for you, of course, *bella mia*," he added, rolling his *l*'s.

When certain Italians speak, it's pure sex. Paolo was one of those Italians. He grabbed me around my rib cage, half lifted me up and then gently dropped me on his leather chaise, wrapping himself around me. Then, like an excited boy, he grabbed my hand, led me to the closet and pulled out a white shirt to try the links on.

"Do you know that cuff links and twins share the same word, *gemelli*?" he asked, sliding around consonants and vowels with his tongue.

"Why?" I asked, just a tad distracted by his accent. "Is it because they mirror each other and are associated with the astrological sign Gemini?" I guessed.

"Yes, sort of." He got serious. "The Latin roots, either *gemellus* or *geminus-gemini*, translate to mean something about being born at the same time, alike, double." He continued. "They are a pair, connected, attached, like us." He was trying to be metaphoric, seducing me with language, culture and jewelry speak, pulling me onto his bed. "I don't think I've ever received a gift that made me feel this special." He held me tightly.

"I'm so glad we aren't conventional. Most women can get to a man through cooking or sex, but I am giving you *gioia* from *gioiello*: similar Latin roots, loosely translated into provoking joy from providing jewels," I said, trying to one-up him with the little Latin and Italian I knew.

"Stop showing off. And, I've tried your cooking; maybe we should stick to sex." He bit my lower lip when he kissed me.

This was the third time I'd been to see him since he moved back to Milan from New York, where we met on a blind date. I'd been in charge of the decorative touches in his completely modernized apartment in a nineteenth-century stone building. In between shopping for throw pillows, sheets and duvets as well as for fabrics for curtains and rugs, he'd taken me to Florence, Sienna, Rome, Orvieto—all beautiful, with enchanting ancient *duomos*, hidden churches with famous art, and violet skies. The part that I truly loved best was helping work out his living space, sleeping till noon, lying in bed and talking about where the furniture would fit—just *being* . . . with *him*.

Before Paolo, the only other jewelry I'd ever given to a guy was one diamond stud earring I took out of my second hole for Billy Fallon, whom I started going out with for a short time in my twenties, after dancing all night with him at Manhattan's Odeon.

Now I'd unexpectedly fallen in love with a man who, in the Italian tradition, called his mother "Mamma." She had given him a carved chest to hold his vast array of cuff links, the taste for which he inherited from his father, as well as some of the ancient Roman intaglios and vintage French enameled styles.

"Most guys have a baseball card collection they've saved. You have a jewelry box," I said when he first took it out proudly to show me.

"I'm from Milan," he teased. "I have taste. I have custom-made shirts."

"You are a peacock and a bit of a snob."

"This coming from the woman who has an entire jewelry armoire?"

Although we ribbed each other, he knew I'd appreciate seeing which cuff links were his favorites and hearing about where they came from: those from his dad, whimsical sets from his brother, more classical looks from his mother, one uninspiring pair from an old girlfriend in France and the Victorian garnet and art nouveau styles he bought himself at antiques markets when he lived in London.

When I gave him the onyx pair, he said, "I've never seen or imagined a treasure such as these." He beamed and admired them on his white shirt, to which we had fastened them.

I'd hoped to bring him this *gioia*, working out various possibilities before deciding on this style. I wanted to give him something completely unique compared to what he already had, something that only I could give to him.

Throughout our years together, I'd done things for him that I'd never done for another man. Hearing that butts look better bronzed from a French friend and knowing his preference for high, heart-shaped *culos*, while mine was flat, small and swiftly being taken down by gravity, I mooned a face tanner and burned my bootie to a crisp. He held me tight, laughed at the story and said my rear was beautiful when it glowed in the dark.

The first time I went to see him, I was over my fear of flying but not over my concerns about crashing, being blown up by terrorists or having a heart attack while spending six out of the nine hours over an ocean. Still I went, with behavioral distraction techniques, Xanax, hope and a bad horoscope for that week. Another time, I had an allergic reaction to a facial treatment, a day before I was leaving. I went to my dermatologist four hours before I was supposed to be at the airport. She sent me to an allergist who talked to me via cell phone while I boarded the plane, ruling out anaphylactic shock even though my lips were swollen like those of a blowfish. She promised that the stress was making it worse and that by the time I landed, it would go down.

After playing with the onyx cuff links, we drove to an out-of-the-way restaurant to continue his birthday celebration. He turned under the same archway six times while cursing with stereotypical Italian hand gestures, and I could no longer stifle my laughter or my suggestion, "Maybe you should try going the other way."

"The problem," he breathed in deeply, "is that there is no other way." One of the traits I loved about him was that he got lost, in the car, on foot, a block from where he lived or on the highway with road maps and large Exit signs. There was something charming, vulnerable and silly about his inability to go in the same direction he came or find his way back to where he started.

"You always like the things about me that drive other people crazy." I didn't care about other people, and by this time in our relationship, I was sure I liked more about him than I had about any other man.

When Paolo and I first met, I was forty-two and serial dating for an article for *More* magazine, on various methods of meeting guys. I hadn't expected to fall in love with him months later, nor had I ever considered a relationship that would consist of my traveling five thousand miles at thirty-five thousand feet, locked in a small space with strangers, heads tilting and falling asleep on my shoulder, every two months.

I was Hurry-Dating, logging on to Match.com, interviewing and being fixed up by two of Manhattan's high-priced matchmakers. I had five or more dates a week and was exhausted, running out of outfits and banter. Most of the men I met were nice, albeit homogenized, versions of the one before, and wrote their profiles with about as much irony as their desire for "romantic walks on the beach at sunset."

Paolo showed up somewhere between my deleting e-mails from married men, twentysomethings and "clean-cut, courteous" bisexuals who all wanted to have an affair, and speed talking with twenty-five guys for three minutes each at Hurry Date.

"Tell him to send me a photo," I said to AJ, whose co-worker was fixing us up.

"Just have a drink with him," AJ said. "You have to be in it to win it."

I agreed to the meeting to stop AJ from quoting Lotto advertising.

On the phone, I immediately liked the way Paolo curled his vowels. I went for Liam because he had a singsong lilt. I was hopeful this accent would prove a better choice.

"I have dark features and will carry the *New York Times* under my right arm."

"Your MO?" I asked.

"My what? What does it mean?"

"Nothing. See you at eight." I was surprised when he showed up.

We fumbled around for conversation for twenty minutes, after he surveyed the lounge-style bar and said quite seriously, "There are way too many men in this place."

"Did you hope to have more choices in women?" I asked, trying to be witty, but it came off sarcastic.

He turned bright red and said, "No! Sorry. I think you are elegant and beautiful, and I was implying there would be a lot of competition for your attention."

He already had it. Although he wasn't traditionally handsome, he was a steamy, exotic mix of French, Egyptian and Spanish on his mother's side and Italian on his father's. He had high cheekbones, full lips, a classical straight nose and large, wide blackish brown eyes that his shaggy brown hair, which needed a cut, kept falling into. He wore Levi's 501s and a cashmere crew neck sweater that suited his boyish five-foot-eleven build.

He was nervous, and it disarmed me. Once the initial tension eased, we found movies, books and art such as the paintings of Piero della Francesca in common. Eventually, drinks turned into dinner. He told me about his childhood in Milan and I confessed to growing up in New Jersey. He tried to seduce me with his knowledge of my favorite type of music (the blues), said my long hands were aristocratic, that my leather jacket was really cool and then, slipping his fingers into mine, he asked, "Do you like to make love in the morning?"

To which I wholeheartedly cracked up, sending him into temporary shock. Even though I apologized, I still had to ask, "Does that work?"

"First time I've tried it," he admitted. It was also the last. I later found out that the one time Paolo could not function on any level was in the morning before taking a brisk walk to the patisserie for an espresso. When we'd have an argument and I wanted to bring it down a notch, this was the line I would use with the best imitation of his accent I could muster. It always worked.

A VP for an international marketing company, Paolo had gone to graduate school in the States. When I met him, it was the third time he had lived in New York. He was married for two years to an American woman, but the relationship fell apart when they both moved to Italy. I let this slide;

a few of my friends who were in great second marriages had had starter ones.

Around a month into it, he said he'd cook for me. Translation: He brought bags of smoked meats and fish, freshly baked breads, olives, cheeses and decadent desserts from a well-known New York City gourmet shop. He laid them out on trays he found in my kitchen, then proceeded to lay me down on the couch and kiss me softly, making me forget time, place and everything else except for what I was feeling in the moment. The idea that the sex could get even better with him as time went on was something I wanted to try out right away, and I invited him over the next night and almost every night after that for the next three months. "I've never felt so secure and confident," he admitted. We danced together to Aretha, Al Green and Sam & Dave in my living room and talked until five a.m. about the deaths of our parents—my mother and father and his father. Then he found out he was being transferred back to Milan by his company and we'd have only another month together.

"Shit. You are going to find someone new as soon as I'm gone." I'd been on twenty-two dates in two months for the article and found that I liked only him.

He left in May and called two days after he got back to Italy and almost every day after that. It was August when he returned for a visit and to talk to old colleagues about finding a job in New York. By the second day, he said he had excruciating pain in his pelvis and looked pasty white. After fourteen phone calls, I got in touch with a urologist at NYU hospital, who told me I had to check his urine to see if we could wait until morning or if we had to go to the emergency room that night. I handed Paolo a paper cup. He refused vehemently. I insisted. Trying to be brave, he teased, "You're a bit of a hypochondriac, so let's go with your opinion." There wasn't enough blood to spend a probable eight hours in an emergency room. The next day we were told he had prostatitis. He was banned from sex and was handed free Cipro. Afterward, he called me bossy. I told him I didn't like him very much. When we slept, he eventually stopped throwing one leg over mine in favor of wrapping himself around me, similar to the way he placed a protective arm around my shoulder on the subway or held my hand when we crossed a street. We sang along to Neil Young, and he said, "We are both really goofy." I liked the way *goofy* sounded with an Italian accent. We were granted our conjugal rights, and he cried on our last night and said, "I've never known this kind of happiness." This was when I fell in love with him and didn't know exactly what to do with it.

"Would you ever think of going to Italy?" AJ asked.

"He hasn't mentioned it and says he is going to try to find a job back here." At the time, I couldn't imagine leaving my niece and nephews, my grandmother, my brothers and friends who had become my extended family. Instead, I found a way to get over three or four times a year. The Italians are a romantic lot. When I told my friends at different jewelry trade organizations about him, they sent me on trips to the jewelry fairs in Vicenza, Arezzo and Naples. I found cheap coach fares, and he came back to New York on Christmas vacations and his August holidays.

By the time his forty-second birthday rolled around, I'd been to Italy nine times. He had sent me his mileage for upgrades to business class. I went with bombs going off in Madrid, heightened security in Milan and Orange alerts in New York. I had his new cuff links made out of Chalcedony gemstones in a subtle violet blue, with tiny deeper blue sapphire accents. On one side, they were round in shape; on the other side, oval—alike but just slightly different, in the same way our relationship had become. I became familiar with his moodiness, and he encountered my overreacting when I felt let down. I made it my mission to get him back to New York, finding headhunters and helping him redo his résumé. He sent me books and CDs he thought I'd like. We had phone "dates" in which we'd listen to music together and talk for three hours as though we were sitting across from each other. "I'm pouring myself a drink now," he'd say.

"But you don't drink alone."

"I'm not alone. I'm with you." He continued to charm me.

Some nights we'd have transatlantic phone sex, but the six-hour time difference was tricky. He was saying, "Good night, beauty," content and sleepy, while I was wide-awake and up for five more hours and for more of him.

By the third year, I went with my heart open, a lighter carry-on bag and less Xanax. When he saw me in Milan, he continued to look at me like the first time we met.

When I was back home, he sent calla lilies with a note when I had two wisdom teeth pulled, orchids to simply say *buona notte*. He sent me e-mails after I'd go over and see him, which were timed for me to read when I landed at JFK.

Finding your mascara, your Coca-Colas in the fridge and even the Prada shopping bag you left, all saddened me. It reminded me of what my regular days are like coming home from work and not finding you here. I miss you deeply and don't know what to do with myself now.

I did.

I made him a birthday present of polished-top rough rubies set into a hammered, almost primitive finish of gold—very ancient and Roman. The pair mirrored each other this time, but I changed the mechanism to allow for one side of both links to detach, so as to be able to move them around more easily. When he saw them he said, "You're brilliant." When I told him I wanted to come to Italy to try a full-time committed relationship, he said, "Stop teasing."

The look on my face gave my hurt away. "Sorry, I didn't mean it to come out like that. But you can't seriously leave your career and all that you have and have built over in the

States for a different country where you don't speak the language and have nothing."

He was making it worse. I thought I had him. And, I had contacts. I had freelance set up. I could still work for the jewelry magazine remotely.

"*Bella*, I'm scared to do it again," he said. "The first time my marriage ended because I had nothing to offer. I travel four days of each week for my job. You will be miserable and hate me in the end. If I were in New York, it would be different."

"But you aren't," I snapped. "As much as I thought you would come back, I now know you're not going to."

He went for the jugular, which happened when he felt cornered. "Every time you're here, you show me where your emergency doctor/call list is and quiz me on what you are allergic to. Do you think you could really live here?"

I dug my nails into my palms to stop from becoming hysterical. "I give you the list because I don't speak the language."

"That's my point." He went to hug me. I backed away.

I got fed up and told him it was over. "I need to find a real, nurturing two-way relationship with someone who is able to get me to a doctor if I am sick"—as I had done for him.

I realized that every time he felt any need from me, he withdrew or snapped at me. I wanted time, space and to figure out how to deal with this information, which of course I had known all along, but to which hope had somehow made me blind. When he had gotten sick, I had changed. I was no longer afraid to be intimate and share my feelings, ask for what I needed or give myself so openly to a man. We had a deep connection, of that I was sure, but I also thought, *If I can change, why can't he?* I went with the long-distance romance because I had believed he would eventually come back. I think there were times he actually believed it himself. I allowed him to feed my fantasy by holding on tighter every time I tried to let go. But now I had to deal with the truth and walk away.

"No. Give me some time to think about it and work it out," he asked. "Please, *bella!*"

Two months turned into another year, and I traveled to Italy in a snowstorm, with seven-hour delays, lost luggage and moonstone cuff links. The shape for the stones was the same—oval—but there were variations and changes in the colors, sometimes more luminescent, other times more opaque. Like him, there were shifts in how and what they reflected, depending on how you looked at them. At first the changeability of the stones intrigued and delighted Paolo, but then he pulled me close and said, "Please don't leave me. You are the one person I can count on, you ground and give me strength and, like these gifts over the years, we will always be *gemelli*, attached, alike, born together."

No longer were his words poetic or seductive.

He had laid out the cuff links on the bed while I was getting ready for my flight. I left a note for him, walked out the door and cried for the next ten hours, much of that time spent in turbulence. I had to reconnect with myself and do my best to disconnect from him and the hope of us as a perfect pair.

CHAPTER 16

Chakra Stones

T WO WEEKS AFTER I returned from Italy, I got out
of my sweatpants, put on a little makeup and
dragged myself out of the house and to a jewelry
launch party. The theme of the store was symbolic motifs
and gemstones that "can be curative or spiritual and have
meanings like rebirth, renewal or can help alleviate mi-
graines," the literature read. As an added perk, the public
relations director had scheduled a tarot card reader. I'd had
only one other reading years earlier at another event, and it
scared the hell out of me. I was told that my career was about
to take off (thus far it's been in a constant but interesting state
of flux) and here it comes, the mind-bending prediction that
my love life would be tumultuous for the next fifteen or so
years. Of course, that part came true. When I just turned
thirty and was given this tidbit, I started to wonder what I

had done wrong in another life, even though I didn't believe in past lives.

On different occasions, to try to get past some of my superstitions, I incorporated methods from various Eastern cultures into my life. Once, on the advice of a doctor, I attempted meditation. For two months, while the rest of my group was discovering the mind/body relationship and realizing certain goals through a higher consciousness, I fell asleep. It seemed, the instructor informed me, that I knew only two states of being: "stressed out" or "conked out."

Years later, a friend suggested feng shui. He had just done his apartment and wanted to give mine a try. After we'd changed the position of sharp-edged tables and added plants and colors to specific areas, he told me that my bathroom was in the worst place it could be and if there was any hope for my love life, I'd have to move. Determined to hold on to my large one-bedroom, I started seeing a new therapist, Debra, and put up a mirror on the bathroom door, keeping it closed at all times to reflect the bad energy back out of the apartment and to keep my option for love open. This was when I met Paolo.

During the weeks after the breakup with him, I'd question everything from my choices in men, fate, timing, my preference for understated lingerie, my bikini wax versus completely bare—and blurted out to Debra (whom I'd now been seeing for five years) that therapy wasn't working anymore. Don't get me wrong—Debra had been a great psychologist. She armed me with the cognitive behavioral techniques to reduce my fears of flying on long trips. She helped me to express my anger and sadness instead of seeking diagnoses for headaches and numbness in my hands and feet. She got me through caring for my father when he had cancer, the grief I finally allowed myself to feel for my mother and my opening up to intimacy. She taught me that the root of many of my superstitions or "catastrophizing" has been my fear of loss, which was present ever since my parents' divorce. But when it came to men, no form of talk or cognitive behavior therapy was helping me find one who wanted to stick around.

At the party, a very attractive Argentinean guy said, "You should go in to see the reader. She's very good." He gave me a little nudge, which had me standing smack in front of her, the table and the cards. I would have preferred to stay outside, trying my luck with him.

Serina introduced herself and asked me to turn over a card. During my five-minute reading, she told me almost exactly what Debra had said for years: "You're standing in your own way. Your negative beliefs could be sabotaging your goals." Then she said, "You must let go of a man with whom you have a deep connection. Then you will be more open to another who is of like mind.

"You can ask one question," she then offered.

Still holding out some hope, I asked, "The man with whom I have this deep connection—is there any time in the future that it could work out—or if I let him go, will it be forever?"

"He will stay in your life as long as you let him. He loves you, but he's not capable of the relationship you want."

"Will he ever be?"

She shrugged. "This is your reading, not his."

"Think about your feelings, not Paolo's," Debra always said.

I'd like to say that the subtext of the party and Serina's Zen-like advice opened me up to a new plan for mixing Western therapy with Eastern spiritual training, but really, it was a newly acquired engraved 18K gold lotus-motif talisman (for new beginnings) that perked me up.

I was able to admit to myself that I was continually trying to ward off bad luck instead of trying to attract good fortune. Even on my trips to see Paolo in Milan, I was convinced that my past twenty some-odd plane rides had been safely guided, not by control towers and careful pilots, but by wearing a thick silver chain dangling with weighty silver amulets. This hefty concoction of pendants comprised charms that my friends and family had given me over the years. The heavy metal made the security beepers go off, and my neck felt as if it should be in traction by the time the plane was on the ground. But (knock on wood) I always landed.

Once, while traveling with Paolo for a romantic weekend from Rome to Venice, I was clutching the "good luck, safe travels" necklace, and he asked, "Are you really going to wear that thing?"

"I have worn it on every trip to see you. Do you really want me to stop now, the first time we are flying together?" I asked as the plane was climbing.

"No, no, you should wear it. Here, let me help you get your hair while you put it on. But you do sort of look like an old Sicilian woman with a modern version of a rosary. You aren't going to start kissing it and praying to the saints?"

After the tarot card experience, it was time to stop indulging my superstitions, to stop clinging to my negative thoughts and what-ifs. I was going to be more open, to do things that invited positive energy into my life. Giving up my aerobics of Latin grooves or sculpt classes at the gym for chanting and meditative yoga was not a sacrifice I was willing to make after working out for years to get my abs and glutes in shape.

In a misguided attempt to feel better, I started purchasing well-designed talisman jewelry from various designers I'd met through my work (rationalizing about spending more than I could afford with the thought that at least the pieces were meaningful and potentially healing rather than just pretty and expensive bandaging). Off went my diamonds and platinum and on went high-karat-gold delicate medallions in graduated length chain. There was the gold lotus leaf medallion for transformations. This would help me forget Paolo and find a commitment-friendly boyfriend closer to home. An etched pendant that resembled Ganesha, the god of strength and fortitude, which promotes success by removing obstacles would help me achieve a more organized living space and would eventually lead to an uncluttered mind. A diamond set Tree of Life, which evokes deeper grounding and faith, was obviously something I needed more of in all aspects of my life. I wore four other charms/pendants that hung at varying lengths with spiritual meanings and motifs.

Reluctant about the rules regarding weakening the power of my new necklaces by taking them off to shower and sleep, I decided not to risk it and woke up every morning for one month to untangling seven chains. Not known for my patience, I was about to retire my "good luck" charms when I noticed they made for an extremely fashionable look. But I still wasn't over Paolo, nor was I any closer to finding a new man, and I still was in an apartment that was "flushing away all [my] chances of love."

I had heard about a day spa close to my apartment that was promoting a treatment to tap into the healing properties of gemstones. The idea of jewels being part of a beauty treatment had me intrigued. The facial and massage were based on the Hindu system of seven chakras (energy points) on the body, representing different aspects of our emotional, spiritual and physical being. "The color of each gemstone relates to the different chakras and is placed on each point for its curative powers," the spa manager explained.

Once on the table, I asked the practitioner if there were any stones for landing a stable, lasting romantic relationship. "Rose quartz on your heart, for compassion and to let love in." She handed me a loose stone to put under my pillow at night for some additional help. While unsure if it all worked, I was reveling in the hot massage and the serene space. For the first time in months, I felt more relaxed, peaceful and content. Upon leaving, I looked at my watch, saw I was running late for an appointment and began to rush . . . face-first into the spa's plate-glass door. To be clear, I am not without my faculties even in the most stressful moments, and I usually take responsibility for my klutziness; however, there were two doors, which had just been cleaned spotlessly, and I still believe anyone trying to hurry might not have noticed the second one either.

"Quite lucky you didn't break it," my ENT doctor said when he agreed to an emergency appointment the same day after my nose had swelled up to three times its size and turned various shades of black, blue and olivine. He informed me that the swelling would likely go down in anywhere from three weeks to two months. With my track record of taking forever in the healing process when it came to men, I had a hunch I was looking at the outside time frame.

I consider myself anything but vain. I run to the grocery store in my neighborhood with my hair in a high Pebbles-style ponytail, no makeup, in my signature sweatpants, which could be misconstrued as pajamas, and once in my actual pajamas while sick to get myself soup. In between my trips to see Paolo, I'd let my roots grow an extra week, even skipped a few waxings, but I couldn't imagine walking around looking as if I'd been KO'd in a boxing match for this questionable length of time and what that would do to my chances of meeting a new man. All I could do was think, *What if it doesn't go down* ever?

On the street, I noticed a guy in front of me grabbing a cab. He asked where I was going and upon finding out I was headed downtown, he suggested we share. During the bumpy ride, in which there was absolutely no way of hiding my black eyes and multicolored nose without wrapping my cashmere scarf around my face like a ski mask, I listened distractedly as he told me that he'd seen me in the medical building elevator, that his name was Bill and that he was an environmental lobbyist. I told him I wrote about jewelry and style for magazines. We were nearing my stop. Finding we lived only a few blocks from each other, he handed me his card and said he'd like to take me to dinner.

"My nose doesn't always look like this." I'm not quite sure why I informed him of this when he'd already asked me for a date.

"Yes, I figured that you somehow bruised it, which I suspected was why you were in the medical building and that no body part could be in a perpetual state of black and blue and is that . . . green?" He opened the door to let me out. I got excited about some new banter in my life.

It was winter and Bill was wearing an overcoat. Superficially, I could only decipher that he had a head full of short light brown soft corkscrew hair, darker brown eyes, an extremely small nose (although I might have thought that about Jimmy Durante on this particular day). His other features were also fine, plain, but he had dimples when he smiled and he wore small glasses that gave him a disarmingly bookish appeal. He was tall and the overall effect was attractive. He was in need of a new scarf, but if he was able to overlook my oversized schnoz and raccoon eyes, I could also ignore his shoes that looked like his dog played tug-of-war with them. And, up until this particular moment, I'd never had a chance meeting that wound up in a potential date. I was immediately taken by the suspension of disbelief that usually only happens in a Nora Ephron film with Louis Armstrong playing in the background. Or maybe, the heart chakra stone or my myriad pendants were working after all. I would never know. On the phone, planning our brunch date when he told me he was fifty with two daughters, I was already imagining a future with his ready-made family, remembering that the tarot card reader had said, "Open yourself up."

I had been sad, my defenses down, my insecurities and neuroses all rising to the surface like a pot about to boil, which was exactly why I was trying different things; hence the "new" nose.

Bill chose an organic (but not vegetarian) restaurant. While listening to his stand on buying locally, how he grew up in Manhattan and loved brisk long runs in Central Park, I couldn't help but think how a fifty-year-old man raised in the heart of New York City could wear high-waisted wide-wale corduroys in chestnut brown, a plaid flannel shirt and a scratchy Shetland wool scarf. When he told me about his ten-year-old daughter Stacy's love for peace-sign jewelry and his twelve-year-old daughter Jacie's first crush on a boy, and when he spoke proudly of their grades, his clothes seemed to fade into the background. He appeared to be a good guy, calm, even-keeled.

There was also a saying on the maternal side of my family: "You can change the clothes, but you can't change the man." Nana Ida told me this while talking about marrying my grandfather, Rubin. He was anything but a smart dresser; yet she knew he loved her, and he became the husband who, for fifty years, would compliment her delicious dinners, tell her she looked beautiful every night upon returning from work and admired the way she kept such a warm home. To the outside world, he allowed it to seem like she was making all the decisions because that was what she needed. She realized this even more so after he died and wished for me a man as good as Papa Rubin.

This theory, however, skipped a generation with my mother when she married my father, who owned approximately four hundred ties, was tailored to perfection and never got a wrinkle in his Armani suits, whether sitting, standing or walking. By the time she met Manny, my stepfather, who wore short-sleeve shirts that made him look like a chemistry teacher, she had learned the Papa Rubin lesson.

She had had enough of style over substance and wanted a guy who was warm and family oriented and whom she could trust. In Manny, she got a good-looking guy, five years younger, who was happy to clean the house, walk the dog and was completely devoted to her and her "three crazy and messy kids." She taught him how to roll up the sleeves on sport shirts and slowly changed his entire wardrobe until he had a sophisticated sense of style to go with his chiseled features.

While sitting with Bill, I thought about my family's traditions and about Paolo, who owned as many ties as my dad and whose taste and shopping sprees seemed to rival my own. I could work with Bill and the no-name ski jacket, bicycle helmet and wool hat with ear flaps. When I asked why he had both, he told me, "You need to cover your ears in winter or you will get sick." This was obviously a lesson taught by his mother, which stuck. On our next date, I overlooked another *outfit* and listened closely for signs while also taking it light and easy. I was genuinely impressed by the time he spent with his family.

He had his daughters four days every other week. "My ex and I are amicable," he said. "We stayed together for many years for the kids' sake, until we thought they were old enough to be able to deal with it. My ex is seeing someone else now, but we thought it best for the girls not to meet him yet." *Smart,* I thought, remembering I was twelve when I had to meet my mother's first boyfriend, George, the French

Canadian. I also realized this would mean it would be a long time before Bill was going to let me be part of his family life, which seemed perfectly okay during our getting-to-know-each-other phase. He was aware of his daughters' feelings, didn't hate his ex and loved his mother. He spent Thanksgiving at his aunt's, surrounded by his brothers and their families and cousins and grandparents—all the makings of what my grandmother referred to as "a real mensch." She got enthused when I told her about him. "Finally, after all this time and all the rotten apples, this could be the one," she said.

Sometimes talking to my grandmother was like a type of exposure therapy, in which I had to face all my mistakes, head-on and at once. She laughed heartily when I told her this, told me she was proud, wanted me to be happy, and held my hand.

By our third or fourth date, I found out that Bill's hobbies were rock climbing, hiking, and camping. I figured since it was November, there was time to divulge that I was a nature girl only when it came to motifs in jewelry. I loved dragonflies and even spiderwebs in 18K gold. But I had an irrational fear of the live creatures. The last time I stayed in a tent I was fourteen, at sleep-away camp. I'm allergic to bees or yellow jackets or both, and have to carry an EpiPen. My exercise consisted primarily of schlepping carry-on luggage through security checks and high-impact dance classes at the gym such as cardio striptease, belly dancing and Zumba.

His vacations were spent skiing at very high altitudes. I

got vertigo while climbing the Spanish Steps in Rome. I had a fear of heights and couldn't imagine being on a tram. He had a fear of women who didn't recycle to perfection. I power shopped at Prada and Dolce & Gabbana in Milan. Bill kept beating his time in the NYC Marathon.

But somehow we managed to work around it because we were still leading separate lives, seeing each other only twice or three times a week when he didn't have his daughters.

I wanted it to work out. This was a guy who was able to commit to a woman (he'd already done it once), two kids, the right school systems and saving trees. Was the fact that none of our hobbies or lifestyles matched really a problem in the big picture? We shared family values, a love for kids and he lived two blocks rather than five thousand miles away. Paolo and I had movies, music, books, taste in fashion, home decor and even jewelry in common. He was able to cry to me and I was able to tell him of my fears. All that got me was a guy who would stay in my life for as long as I let him but who could never give me a committed long-term relationship.

Still, by the third month, Bill had no idea of my neuroses, such as the fact that I hated sitting in the balcony in movie theaters and that I needed to have the aisle seat. I felt motion sickness every time I went to see a film with him. He knew nothing of my insomnia, superstitions or fear of loss. He didn't ask. I didn't tell. Although I hadn't met either of his daughters (Bill thought it was too soon), I made one a beaded turquoise bracelet, which she had heard to be good for luck; she needed to ace this basketball season. He made me locally farmed dinners.

"He's too healthy for me," I told Debra. "I'm bored."

"It's not because he's healthy, but because you have nothing in common and you are not being who you really are." I noticed that when we went to the movies, he only got the first layer; he couldn't go deeper. Any further discussion would cause him to pull me close and kiss me and get him all riled up for sex. I was less enthused. I needed mental stimulation. He became predictable, like the hum of the refrigerator, or perhaps soothing, like mashed potatoes, comfort food.

Eventually I began to notice that he was not as together as I thought. He kept all the different aspects of his life completely compartmentalized: his daughters, his outdoor hobbies, his guy trips, his work, and then came me—none of these components of his life ever got mushed together. We had been together five months, and I felt like an adjunct to his life.

One weekend when I was away with my niece and nephew, I realized when he e-mailed rather than called, that he needed to keep me at a distance, never really allowing me into his world. When I got home, I explained what I was feeling. He said he'd change it so we could be together and it got worse—sporadic calls, canceled dates, until finally I ended it. Or thought I did.

Two weeks later, an e-mail arrived while I was away on a business trip. *Want to see a movie this weekend? The girls are away with their mom.* I was flummoxed by his attempt at seeing me and talked to my magazine editor, a younger married guy and a friend, who knew just enough about my love life and my writing style. "You are very much a dot-dot-dot person. That leaves everything open to interpretation. It's time to use declarative periods at the end of your sentences. He will get the point."

I never heard from him again. Paolo kept texting, though.

While I was happy that I'd ended something that was going nowhere within a reasonable amount of time and with my heart still intact, I was also glad that I had had a relationship (albeit a short one) with a guy who was, for all intents and purposes, nice and easy. It helped me get my balance back. He was the equivalent of my version of meditation. I wasn't stressed out, but I finally conked out.

I hadn't even noticed that my nose was completely normal or that I didn't feel my heart in my feet every time I heard the text message signal on my cell.

I'm still happy with my talisman pieces, although I don't wear all seven together anymore. And, just in case the chakra facialist was right, I continue to sleep with a rose quartz under my pillow.

CHAPTER 17

To Catch a Thief Jewels

"WHERE DID YOU stash the diamonds?" my grandmother Ida whispered in my ear. Dressed in a sky blue cashmere sweater that matched the color of her eyes, a thin gold filigree cuff bracelet, a strand of gray pearls and small gold clip earrings, Nana Ida wore a pale lipstick and a hint of blush that she still called rouge. Two months earlier she'd turned ninety-four, cropped her hair short and let the last hint of blond wash out in favor of salt-and-pepper. "It's much better to go natural with makeup and hair at my age and accessorize more." She squeezed my hand. I looked around the nursing home and noticed some of the other residents: They were also without jewelry or "rouge" and dressed in mismatched clothing or pajamas. I found comfort in the fact that my grandmother still took pride in how she looked and made an effort every day. This wasn't vanity. It represented her will to live and her ability to make the most of any situation, like her move from her brightly decorated one-bedroom apartment with separate living room and kitchen in the independent living facility to the nursing home, where she shared a small dorm-size space with a roommate.

She walked me around, introducing me to the nurses, one of whom said, "Your grandmother is one strong and tenacious woman."

"It's a kinder way of saying bossy," my grandmother said, laughing, still knowing exactly who she was. She also remembered that I had recently gotten rid of the guy who hadn't deserve me and that I'd just returned from Paris. And on this particular visit, she believed I was an international jewel thief.

My grandmother had been diagnosed with an atypical and slowly progressing type of dementia two years earlier. She would sometimes forget what time or day of the week it was, but she always recognized and knew her family, and she could retell in vivid detail stories that dated back seventy years. She'd retained her sharpness and wit. But every now and then, certain everyday truths went a bit askew. It seemed the new freelance career she thought I was involved with could facilitate obtaining the jewelry on the wish list that she handed me.

"No, not the diamonds you took from that couple in Paris," she said without a hint of judgment. "These are just some costume pieces like those I saw on *The View* and would like you to get for me at the mall." As I skimmed the list she had handed me, the items were definitely in the top trends: longer necklaces, a new cocktail ring or two and larger textured link chains in yellow gold for her wrist.

I immediately phoned her neurologist, who said, "It could definitely be much worse." Worse than thinking I stole from the friends I was staying with in Paris? As the words came out of my mouth, I realized that he was right. She still knew I was her granddaughter, complained on cue about what I was wearing and proudly introduced me to everyone we saw. So what if she told her dinner companions something to the effect of "My granddaughter knocked over the Victoria and Albert Museum and is hiding the crown jewels"? Her doctor said, "She usually can determine what she's imagined from reality in around a week. You don't want to agitate her, so it's best to go along with the fantasy. You want to make the most of your visit with your grandmother. It will be okay."

I took his advice. I told her about my breakup with Paolo, to which she said, "Good riddance—time to find someone who is not emotionally stunted and lives in the United States. Also, possibly you want to look around for someone who is straight, single, neither a struggling writer nor failing actor, and probably best if he wants to marry you too." Somehow the disease has not affected her ability to whip off all my failed romances in five minutes flat. "Bethy," she says, using the name she calls me when about to engage me in a serious chat, "I just want to see you happy and settled. You deserve it. Do you know that? Find a nice guy who'll love you and appreciate you and your big heart." It continued.

"And maybe if you didn't come looking like you were on your way to the gym, you could meet a nice doctor here." I am relieved that for the first time on that day, I knew exactly what was going to come next. She put on her glasses, looked me over and asked, "What the heck are you wearing? Did you forget you were coming to visit me?" It doesn't matter that I was in Juicy Couture, a perfect shade of slate gray velour with fitted hoodie and wide-leg bottoms. To my grandmother, the woman whose rule was never to leave the house (and who now doesn't go into the dining room) without lipstick or earrings, "A sweat suit is just that! And should be worn only to do laundry, go for a run or to work out in a fitness center."

When I was growing up and Nana Ida and I were sharing confidences, we'd also get "all dolled up"—two dressed-up ladies lunching on fish sticks, macaroni and cheese and real chocolate pudding we pulled out of little glass doors at the Horn & Hardart Automat in New York City. I counted on her for guidance, grounding and constancy when my parents got divorced and throughout most of my life. During my preteen years, my grandmother was the person I most liked to spend New Year's Eve with; I couldn't wait to get to my grandparents' house in Brooklyn. She brought out her best crystal, and we'd pretend that ginger ale was champagne and clinked in the New Year. I would dress up in one of her beautiful lace and silk nightgowns and empty out her jewelry box, finding the pieces she had scored while scouring the pawnshops and secondhand stores and traveling through Europe—the perfect combination of real and faux jewelry. I'd mix wide art deco diamond bracelets with long strands of glass beads and chokers worn like a tiara in my hair. I would lay everything out neatly on her bed and decide on my grandmother's adornments as well, always making sure we were both glistening from every angle in piled-on jewelry.

These times spent with Nana Ida fueled my ongoing attraction to period pieces, layering pendants and stacking rings and bangles. Sometimes we'd Lindy or twist the night away in our get-ups. During other visits, I would watch *NBC Saturday Night at the Movies*, which allowed me at a very young age to try to emulate style-setting actresses in their iconic roles. I was at my grandmother's the first time I ever saw Grace Kelly looking so poised and elegant in *To Catch a Thief*, the day after which we went to Woolworth's to purchase a rhinestone version of the bib-style diamond drop necklace that she wore while seducing Cary Grant. I went back and forth between singing "Diamonds Are a Girl's Best Friend" and nonchalantly saying, "Personally, I think it would be tacky to wear diamonds before I'm forty," which Audrey Hepburn taught me as Holly Golightly in *Breakfast at Tiffany's*. These moments were magical and helped me to escape the growing pains of adolescence: whether the boy of the moment would like me, the realization that my parents were never getting back together, my father's impending marriage, my mother's wearing my jewelry and going to EST and my new silver braces that had glinted rather than sparkled every time I opened my mouth. Our deep connection was built primarily on love and understanding but also on our affinity for jewelry and my grandmother's teaching me how to make life more glamorous. "When you go out looking your best, the rest of the world won't know how you are feeling, even if your heart is breaking," she had told me.

Fifteen years before, when we lost my mother on that humid July day, our five yearly visits grew into ten. When my grandmother was in her eighties and could still travel, I'd have her come up from her home in Fort Lauderdale and stay with me in my small Manhattan apartment, going on museum outings and to off-Broadway shows. We'd talk five times a week, both craving continuity and closeness. On Mother's Day, my mom's birthday and the anniversary of the day she died, we talked about everything but that: the grief, always palpable but unspoken. Instead, we'd discuss my brothers' wives' neuroses, Ethel's grandson's divorce, Judith's hip replacement, whether I thought it might be time to lighten up my hair.

From the time she used to babysit me, I took on some additional traits to those genetically inherited such as making a short story longer and being a grown-up since I was a kid (Nana Ida was the oldest sister too). On our last visit she confided, "You are my best friend. No one has ever under-stood me as much as you, nor have I ever had as much fun."

She pulled me close and in a hushed tone, asked again, "So, hurry up and tell me—where did you stash the dia-monds?"

"Safety deposit box, seemed the best place till I can . . . fence them," I said in my best cat burglar speak. The safety deposit box was actually where I keep her pieces, mostly those with sentimental value: a large circular pendant she was awarded for her charity work, marcasite pins with my grandfather's and her initials entwined in script. There were also certain pieces left over from what was once part of a fifties-style charm bracelet that dangled and spun around her wrist to reveal her favorite keepsakes: a heart and key locket with a photo of my grandfather, my and my brothers' names engraved onto 14K male and female plaques, souvenirs picked up on travels from around the world, which she col-lected to always remember the beautiful places and people she had seen and met. The bracelet was broken up years earlier, some charms given to her favorite nieces and friends as mementos. Prior to that, she sold all of what she deemed her "good" pieces to help with the down payment on my grandparents' Florida condominium, where they moved during my late teens.

When she was diagnosed with dementia, I held on tightly, trying to keep things as normal as possible. I continued to ask her for advice about the guys in my life, to gossip with her about my sisters-in-law. Growing up in a time when warned that dented cans could cause botulism, she was very definitive in her response to my inquiry of whether she thought I would look better with a bit of Botox. "The lines on your forehead show that you laughed, cried and lived. And when I actually can see them on yours, I am sure they will add more character to your face." She eschewed "fancy anti-aging serums" and believed Pond's Cold Cream was the multipurpose key to a freshly cleansed and smooth appearance and that a smile does more to enliven your face than any line diminisher or piece of jewelry.

Then there were the days she confided in me that she went to medical school (never) and that she was dancing with many tall men at the Rainbow Room (the night we moved her into the nursing home). But she continued to say things to let me know it was still her. Two days into my visit with her at the nursing home, I called my grandmother on the way to the mall and told her, "I'm shopping for what you need and will be there to see you in two hours, give or take."

"Oh good. I really need to dress up the pink twin set and the gray silk. Just go to Claire's," she advised. I lingered over the elongated Diamonds-by-the-Yard station necklaces and the wide link bracelets, trying to choose the ones that looked the most real, most elegant and dramatic, most like my grandmother. I put them in an unassuming black drawstring bag and brought them to her as if they were loot from the heist.

She hugged me tightly. "I'm so glad you came for a visit.

Please come more often. I feel like a forties movie star," she said as she fastened and draped the pieces I just bought around her neck and wrists.

A new nurse passed. My grandmother introduced me. "This is my granddaughter. She writes about jewelry and style for magazines." Her grasp on reality was back as the doctor said it would be. I took out two inexpensive crystal champagne glasses I had bought at Crate & Barrel and poured fizzy ginger ale. We toasted to us and to life, always more glamorous.

CHAPTER 18

Vintage Gems

WHEN I RETURNED from visiting my grandmother, I thought about my new dilemma, which was twofold: how to wear my antique jewelry without looking like an antique and how to get guys from my decade to look at me. It seemed I was becoming too old for a relationship with men who were oh, like, around, my age. They had begun to view me as vintage, not in the same way as a fine wine or fast car but more like a dried prune or broken-down Chevy. I was double-obsessing: Did my grandmother's once-chic heirlooms make me look like an older woman born in her era rather than a modern purveyor of all things classically chic? Did my contemporary male counterparts want a more hip version (read: *much* younger model)? Had I myself become retro?

This all came on like a perimenopausal hot flash one day

while I was multitasking—flipping through fashion magazines, writing an article on buying estate jewelry and perusing profiles on Match.com. The publications and Match suggested that during the years I was off seeing Paolo—who liked the way my forehead crinkled and my nineteenth-century necklace graced my neck—dating appropriate men and wearing jewelry that would not date me had become a new skill I would have to master.

I had not been on Match.com since writing the dating article for *More* magazine five years earlier. I thought I had learned the secret language of the online dating world and that the article had made me a pro—not so much at landing the guy or closing the deal on a wedding ring, but at least at getting me out there to meet and maybe discover some new possibilities. In my research of the covert codes of cyber mating, I had found a few things worthy of sharing: The men whose profiles say they shop at Home Depot usually have wives who have sent them there; "love doing cultural things" translated into seeing any film with Seth Rogan in it; "dry and acerbic" usually means depressed and on Zoloft. And most important, if you talk more than ten minutes or e-mail more than twice, your expectations would be raised so much that meeting Colin Firth would be a disappointment. We've all discovered that athletic means chubby and that open to a relationship means they are good for a hookup. Although I sussed much of this out within the first few weeks of reading profiles for the article years before, I did rack up dates with many nice men who all seemed to blend into the Mr. Maybe or Mr. Not-at-All categories.

Once I had ended it with Paolo and found my romance with Bill to be as exciting as shopping for batteries, I signed back on to Match.com for what Debra, my therapist, and AJ both advised should be an adjunct to my dating life. I wasn't aware that I had a dating life to add to, but let's not get finicky about small details. I rolled my eyes, made horsey snorting sounds and generally pooh-poohed the entire idea. But AJ pulled his "You have to be in it to win it" line on me again, and my therapist channeled my grandmother and said something to the effect of, "It can't hurt. Give it a try. It only takes one."

I pondered my other problem: Was I wearing the appropriate jewelry at this stage in my life? I did not want to look like I was trying to emulate my niece or to come off looking like I was ready for the retirement home. I gave advice on these topics of jewelry and relationships; yet how to meet the right man was still a mystery to me, and it was messing with my confidence in my personal style.

I'd been known to give up pieces of clothing earlier than necessary so as not to look as if I was trying too hard. Even though my legs are perhaps my best feature, I gave up miniskirts in my thirties. When they came back into style a couple of years ago, I enjoyed the irony of friends raising their hemlines while lifting their foreheads.

Jewelry seemed to have a longer life span, although once

I entered my forties, I gracefully retired my toe ring. Next went my ankle bracelet, although I might have been a tad hasty as my ankles were the only part of my body that hadn't started to droop, drop, sink or sag. Every now and then I get a little wistful for the diamond heart that used to dangle from a chain and seductively graze the top of my foot, much in the way I think back to when I had a first date who looked longingly at me.

No matter how many sitting or standing crunches I did, I could no longer pull off my delicate belly chain without looking like an aging Las Vegas stripper.

Instead, I opted for double drop earrings or slightly longer pendant earrings to detract from the crow's-feet around my eyes, as these were much more forgiving than a pair of larger hoop earrings that emphasized rather than camouflaged the dreaded droop of the lobes. At one time or another in my forties, each and every one of my body parts seemed to want to fall down. I was trying to rev myself up to log back on for the possibility of love, and while renewing my subscription to Match, I tried to remember some other important tidbits, such as why some men think that shirtless is a good look for their profile picture.

AJ, who was divorced eight years earlier and doing online dating too, told me to stop procrastinating and overthinking it and upload a few new photos from "this year."

Yes. I had done this before. I recalled that every man's profile I had scrolled through while writing the article had read something to the effect of: *Please have a recent photo in which I can see your face and your entire body. Why not have a few close-ups and full-lengths, preferably not in black-and-white or grainy sepia tones. Perhaps you might like to take a new one today and upload it. If you Photoshop and I can tell, you will not hear from me.* Okay, I exaggerate a bit. I understood their need to know what women looked like currently, and that is exactly what I would give them: an up-to-date, unretouched photo. However, I would not smile, as that would show laugh lines, now called nasolabial folds.

Once all was uploaded, I asked for a *new* photo back ("fair is fair"), sans baseball cap. I got tough and also wrote: *I understand this means your hairline is receding or has receded, but please note that your favorite team hat will only emphasize that you are trying to hide this fact. Would Ed Harris do that? And please, I do not need to see a photo album of shots from your life, including your high school graduation leading up until today. If you must, put that on Facebook. It will not have the desired effect of getting me so confused I think you still might be the guy at your ten-year reunion rather than your thirtieth. Please do not be wearing snorkeling gear or ski masks. Write instead that you like outdoor sports.* After I wrote this but did *not* post it, I decided to take more of a participatory, assertive role and not wait for e-mails to find me, but to surf the site, something I hadn't really done the first time around because I had received an onslaught of e-mails the first week and ongoing messages for the next. But that was five years ago. I was older. There had been nothing in my in-box in six days.

My metabolism had gone on a prolonged strike, and I upped my gym schedule from four to six days a week, doubling cardio and weight workouts, and wearing a heart rate/fat/calorie-burning monitor to find that my two-hour, back-to-back sessions had burned exactly 248 calories when I should have been burning at least 700. I found that maintaining toned abs and glutes turned into a second full-time job; I took it on so that I could feel just a wee bit comfortable while taking off my clothes in dim lights in front of a new man, but then I was smacked in the head with the realization that I could not for the life of me get even a "wink" from a new man.

This is just one of the challenges about growing older alone—the person you meet now (if you are lucky enough to actually meet someone) will not retain the vision of you all toned and taut and smooth, because he has never seen you like that. This will be the first time he is seeing you, and first impressions, God help me, do last. So, while I was horrified to think about all of this, what freaked me out more was that I finally started to receive e-mails—from men who were older than my stepfather (sixty-seven), guys who looked like Truman Capote and those who wrote, *I have a full life, four adult kids, and am now semiretired and have moved to the Midwest to write a screenplay.*

Where were the guys in my designated demographic, age span of forty-six to fifty-eight, single, divorced, widowed, kids, pets, living in San Diego or Sweden? I honestly thought that I was keeping my options open, that these qualifications were quite reasonable, and for a forty-seven-year-old woman, I was flexible much in the same way I was able to switch from yellow to pink to white gold or platinum from colored gemstones to diamonds as long as the particular style was either sophisticated or playful and suited my personality. Yet much to my chagrin, AJ had identified the problem: I was not turning up in these men's searches.

"Why?" I asked. Hadn't I allowed for a wide range of men?

"Guys our age are looking for younger," he said quickly, trying to deliver just the information and move on.

"Duh," I said. "I live in this century." As far as jewelry, if it's over a certain age, one of a kind, retained as much as possible in its original condition, it's considered more valuable. Not so in the case of the way my "ideal man" viewed me. Sometime in the past five years I had become simply older, and there were more current models to be found. Although I consider myself a realist, I continue to be consistently hopeful when it comes to romance and still believe that if I do everything right, it will all work out and I will find a guy to love me, natural flaws and all. But I am also wise to the fact that men facing their mortality look for women who are still solid, with everything high and round, because this will inevitably lead to these guys feeling like they will be able to woo women forever no matter what shape they themselves are in.

"You've got it wrong," one of my guy friends who was also my ex-doctor and my age told me. "It's more simplistic. Younger women look better." He then made me a "flow-chart" of female and male maturity crossing and said something about my liking older boys when I was in high school (which I didn't), which gives men every right and biological imperative to go for girls half my age now. It put the clichéd *expiration date* in an entirely new perspective when he said, "Basically, you look great now, but you are on borrowed time."

Saying this to a woman of a certain age is one thing; saying it to a woman, once your patient, and a slight hypochondriac, is quite another story. I began to hyperventilate over lunch, to which he was treating me to celebrate my *birthday*. I shrugged him off as a good diagnostician and rethought the whole friendship-with-an-ex-doctor thing.

I remained steadfast in my belief that if a man my age or thereabouts met a woman my age whom he found attractive, funny, independent, he might consider her a prospect to at least meet and have coffee with. I tried to compare it to how I admired the qualities of an art deco bracelet with its unexpected details and hidden nuances and the value that age brings to the piece just as I thought I could bring value to a relationship—in man speak, like a goddamn vintage Ferrari. So why couldn't they see it?

AJ came to my rescue and tried to curtail my rant and get me back into cyberspace. "Lie!" he said. "You look much younger than you are. You are attractive and in great shape. Do what every other woman and man on the site does and take five or six years off your age!"

Had I wanted to do that, I would have gone to Demi Moore's doctor and dispensed with the drama of dishonesty and instead gone out with younger guys. I actually did this the first time around and wasn't very good at it.

Dan was thirty-six to my forty-two. By the third date, he wanted to have sex and thought it strange that I still was not ready. I might have been game, but I wanted to take it slowly because he was good-looking, tall, funny, smart and single, leading me to be skeptical about what he saw in me. I wanted a meaningful relationship, and he was six years my junior. I threw caution to the wind on our fourth date, had sex and found it to be the worst experience I'd ever had—one that would not get better with time, although I tried to believe it could; but with age comes wisdom. There was no way that during our one night, his acting like an airplane coming in for a landing was going to do it for me. I'd overcome a fear of flying. Propeller sounds would never be titillating. So the next day, I said, "I think with our age difference, it's probably best to be friends," with a straight face and more guilt for having made up a cockamamie excuse, exactly what I had never wanted done to me.

"But wait. You were worried I didn't like you, and now you acted just like a guy. You basically humped and dumped me."

I tried a twenty-four-year-old on a number of friends' recommendations. "It's fun!" He was gorgeous and I had absolutely nothing in common with him. So for our date, I suggested bowling and then asked if he might like a hot chocolate afterward. Mrs. Robinson, I was not.

Back to this dating round. I told AJ I was not falsely advertising.

"But Beth, you were forty-one, twice." It was true I had been one year younger for several years now, but it was such a blip that no one except AJ and Sammie noticed—not even my brothers.

Being forty-seven instead of forty-eight seemed so reasonable that even I had forgotten.

"But won't it be more appealing if a guy finds me to look better than my years rather than to question them?" I asked.

"Sure, but that would be if they were willing to meet you." Logic was not fitting into this equation; yet I still was in no way writing that I was forty-two.

I was taking a stand for all the alfalfa-sprout-eating women with personal trainers and rock-hard stomachs and legs like Madonna that were being left out of the "search" because of a number.

After another week, I found that younger guys were contacting me again. I began scanning profiles of the guys my age more carefully and found that my "ideal matches" thought they were being subtle in their approach to advertising for younger women.

Most thought they were clever while trying to get their point across in their profiles. At the top of one it read *Age: forty-five. Looking for women between the ages of eighteen and thirty-five.* Then there was some hooey about *a love of moonlit walks on the beach* and a desire for a woman who looked good in *everything from jeans and a T-shirt to a little black dress,* the dissertation on the *Current Photo* and then way at the very bottom of *About Me—I am really fifty-eight, not forty-five, hahaha, LOL, but I wanted to make sure to get into the search of the eighteen- to thirty-five-year-old woman I want to date.*

I stared at the computer. AJ came over. I showed him. "It gives him a wider audience," AJ said.

"Hello . . . The guy is basically saying he won't date anyone in his age group and, moreover, he really thinks that an eighteen-year-old might look at him even though he's fifty-eight? Do you do this?" I asked.

"No. But I'm divorced, have kids and like women our/ your age." He wrapped his arm around my neck in a playful stranglehold.

"Why again, didn't we marry when we were thirty?"

"Because I married someone else."

"Sure, story of my life."

"Shut up. We became best friends because you felt 'too comfortable' dating me, remember?"

"Yes, and you shut up."

I scrolled through more men.

"Oh look—he's not bad. An architect. Tall, self-deprecating.

Loves *It Happened One Night*. Two young daughters, talks so sweetly about them. *Women between the ages of thirty to forty-eight.*" Okay, I would just make the cutoff. Then it appeared. farther down in *About Me*: *I am fifty but I look much younger and am in better shape than anyone fifty. I run the marathon. I eat healthy. I don't look fifty.*

"You do too," I said, starting to talk to the computer screen. "But maybe if you hadn't written it three times, I wouldn't have thought about it." I logged off.

And then I went out with two thirty-somethings, perhaps for spite, but more so because they'd set up a date with me, and I also feared reverse age discrimination.

These guys seemed to like that my biological clock no longer woke me in the middle of the night and that I was independent and outgoing. Plus they didn't know I was playing beat the clock with gravity, but only because I kept my clothes on.

Then, just like when you begin seeing someone new and your ex comes back, I started to go out with the younger men and the "ideal group" started to contact me. I set up a few dates with guys forty-nine, fifty-three and fifty-one, respectively.

In deciding what to wear, I pulled out a couple of brooches from around the 1930s, and, to give them an updated but still-elegant look, I scattered them on the shoulder of a sweater, offering a flirtatious air. I fastened one to the side of my hip on a little black dress, offering a dash of whimsy.

Then, feeling a bit bohemian, I threw on a seventies-style long magnifying glass pendant and then hoped I didn't look like a seventy-year-old leftover hippie.

I tried to have a little fun with one fifty-three-year-old guy who was full of himself as well as full-bodied and asked why his profile gave an age range of twenty-seven to thirty-eight. He said he liked the way he could still amaze them. I get this part, but then I asked, "Do you want to have more kids?" He had two in college and one who just started law school.

He said, "Of course not."

"Do you think these women might?" I asked ever so nonchalantly.

It hit him after being online for six months. "Oh, so that's why they aren't answering me?" I could think of a few other reasons but didn't say them.

I had a few more clunkers. My favorite was a guy who must have reevaluated asking me for coffee and a chat when at forty-nine, his desired range was twenty-one to thirty-three. He called to tell me that he e-mailed too soon. "I'm really not ready to date yet. So I just called to let you know I won't be calling you."

"So, what's the problem?" AJ asked. "You've complained since high school that men don't call when they say they will."

"What kind of lunatic calls to tell you they're not ready to date yet?"

There was also the guy who sat on his cell phone, trading all through dinner, and then when the couple sitting beside us struck up a conversation with me, he said I wasn't paying enough attention to him. Then he got angry when I wouldn't go home with him. "We would've been great together, babe," he said as I leaped into oncoming traffic to hail down a cab.

"You can't blame a guy for trying," AJ noted.

In the midst of all this madness, I noticed it was no longer winter, and I started to wear my favorite jewelry for warm weather: a bunch of fun mixed-up bangles climbing up my wrist. It seemed no matter how many days you worked out at the gym, something inexplicable happened to your triceps in winter. My chisel instructor handed me ten-pound weights, which I could hardly hold, much less lift over my head. I opted for the seven-point-fives and got to work. He tried to pinch and couldn't grasp anything. Phew. When I go sleeveless, the only part of my arms I want jangling are the piles of bracelets accessorizing them.

Then I went to my dermatologist for a rash caused by a sensitivity to a new product I was using. While prescribing a topical cortisone cream, he asked quite frankly if I wanted to have a little Botox while he gently pulled the middle of my neck.

I asked for a mirror immediately. Although I refused to have him jab my jugular with botulism, I'd obviously missed obsessing over a body part. Unlike Nora Ephron, I had up until that moment not "felt bad about my neck." About my glutes, my abs, my eyes and my forehead, yes, but in my lighting at home, my neck was still graceful and swanlike; but then I saw it had turned into chicken skin before properly baked. This has been my favorite area to bejewel with pendants and necklaces, layered, long, short, vintage and new. Oh, what the heck. I logged off Match and launched back into my life.

I'd always wondered what was wrong with me as a default, I suppose because I could never fix the guy or the relationship and it would be easier if all I had to fix was me. Now I was finding there really was something wrong, or at least askew. The irony of getting healthier mentally and ready for a real relationship is not only finding out that it gets harder to meet the opposite sex when you are older, but discovering that you have to now compete with someone quite similar to your less-together self, women like you were twenty years ago. And the truth is, I am happier about me now, although the situation truly stinks.

I keep my heart open because there might be someone out there who appreciates the rare qualities I find in antique jewelry—the character as well as the inherent beauty of the inclusions and flaws found in gems that get more interesting and alluring over time. I've noticed that modern jewelers are taking their cue from this concept and are reviving ancient elements. They opt for artfully shaped baroque pearls instead of perfectly formed ones and rough cut diamonds with personality and life and some natural nicks and scratches.

A good friend and designer, Todd Reed, thirty-six, ador-able, straight, brilliant and a pioneer in launching elegantly raw diamonds into the fine jewelry business, asked me to be in a promotion for him in *Town & Country* as his favorite cli-ent, with my photo and a short interview. He said it was because I was "beautiful, passionate, make connections with people and 'get it'" and that I am "seriously sexy."

God bless young guys who create ageless jewelry. And having my picture full-blown in *T&C* beat uploading it on Match.com any day.

CHAPTER 19

The Pendant

I DECIDED TO take a break from dating, but not to blow off men altogether. There were two guys who thought I was funny and cool, even though I wasn't in their age demographic. They never noticed new crow's-feet and thought that preparing mac and cheese was cooking. They never judged my appearance even when I was in sweatpants or when I went without lipstick or cover-up as long as I played War with them. They did mind, however, when I talked during football season and that I didn't understand a "corner blitz."

"If you're not watching, then please move out of the way and sit down with us," Dylan, my youngest brother David's son and my eight-year-old nephew said.

"Your head is in the way," Robert, ten, my brother Eric's son, agreed. "Be quiet and root for the Jets."

"Dolphins," Dylan shouted.

"Two men fighting over me. I love it." I got a laugh as I squished in between them and I was transported back to when my brothers used to watch sports together, scream at the TV and tell me to get out of the way.

David and Kim, my sister-in-law, married in their late twenties, a year after my mother died, and had Sammie, my niece. Soon after, Eric, the middle child, followed in his late thirties, marrying Nadine, four years older than me. She had Robert at forty-three, when I was thirty-nine, giving me hope there was still a shot for me. Dylan came two years after, providing Sammie with a brother and Robert with a boy cousin. Also, my niece and nephews have the same birth order and age differences as my brothers and I.

My nephews continued to yell at the players, jumping up and throwing pretzels and chips at each other. When I watch them, I see my brothers growing up all over again. Yet, unlike their dads, they are much easier on me and are impressed that I can shoot hoops, know all *Star Wars* trivia and listen to Kanye West with them. If only it could be so easy with guys who are around my age and are not related to me.

The first three years spent with Sammie alone, I never imagined, with the exception of having my own children, that I could love another person so deeply and unconditionally. Then they arrived, two new kids to play with and protect, to talk to on their level, to be myself with, with no agenda but to open my heart all over again.

Robert came into the world in constant motion. By the time he was two, he could unlock front doors and escape from any apartment or house and make a run for it, all in less than four minutes. He was quick, mischievous and fearless; he tried to fit keys into CD players, put on the shower fully dressed to wash his kitten and emptied out non-childproof drawers into laundry baskets. If they had smaller items like lingerie or socks, he'd scatter them from one room to the next. He was a handful like Eric, but Robert finally grew out of it, and I'm not quite sure my brother ever did. I was given the role of co-godmother although I think I should have gotten full billing. Robert was born in Manhattan, and I made it to the hospital before anyone else, in under fifteen minutes from the time my brother called to say he had arrived, even before Nadine made it out of the delivery room. As Robert got older, he grew calmer, more affectionate, becoming a straight-A student and sportsman who also liked to read, go to bookstores and museums, and to swim in the ocean with me. He was and still is a great date.

Dylan arrived with a smile, the most cuddly and easygoing of all the kids. He warmed to me quickly, maybe because he could tell that his sister liked me or because I'd sneak him out of his crib and let him watch TV with me in the early mornings when he wanted to know what was stirring in his house. When I'd visit him in Indiana, he began asking to come to the airport when he was three and has never stopped. I switched from playing Beauty and the Beast with his sister to being Robin to his Batman and wearing capes and tight tiny masks and playing football with him in the house. He looked out for me, telling me, "You know you can just pretend and wear the mask on top of your head instead of letting it squish your face."

At fifty pounds, he told me, "I can't tackle you as hard as I do Dad. You are a girl, and you will get hurt." He was and still is easy to please and hard to resist.

After the boys were born, I had three kids whom I adored, and although I missed and sometimes grieved not having my own, I was happy they were so much a part of my life and hoped they always would be.

When Kim found out she was pregnant with a boy, Sammie wanted to be the one to call and tell me she was having a brother, and asked, "What's it like?"

"Great. You get to worry about them and take care of them for the rest of your life, and they always appreciate it and look up to you." David, then thirty-five, mimicked gagging.

When Dylan turned five and Sammie ten, she said, "You promised you'd never lie to me, and you did. It's horrible having a brother. They pull your hair, try to play with your friends, don't want to go where you like to eat, and it's impossible to shop with them."

I wondered if omission in this circumstance was the same as fibbing. "Okay, maybe I left out a few parts, but it gets better when you get older; then they just pull your hair." She laughed and told me she really loved Dylan, but he was a true pain in her butt.

"Imagine having to deal with two brothers, both younger."

"Like if Dylan and Cousin Robert were around all the time too. God, no," she laughed.

"Exactly," I said, referring to her father and uncle, but feeling it was much more fun with the two still short, young, skinny and most important guys in my life.

In the early days, the sibling rivalry was replicated. Eric thought I loved Sammie more than Robert, just as he thought my dad felt more for me than him. David was worried I wouldn't have the relationship with Dylan I had with Sammie because he was a boy. He had heard and obviously had been affected by the story of my wanting to exchange him for a sister when he was born. My brothers and I might have been replaying patterns, but the kids all knew how much they meant to me, and if they ever needed a little proof, they were smart enough to up the ante on their birthday and Christmas gifts.

As I sat between Robert and Dylan, pretending to understand the football game still going, Robert says, "Hey, is your hair lighter? It looks good."

"Nope," I tell him, "the same." Dylan gets in on the compliments, pointing to my high black boots worn over my jeans, and says, "Those are really cool."

Then Robert gets to what's been on his mind, blurting out, "I have a girlfriend and need some advice."

"From Dylan or me?" I ask.

"Funny," he says.

Then Dylan jumps into the conversation. "I have one too, and her name is Natasha."

I'm excited by the role of confidante, notice that male competition in my family is still alive and can't wait to hear more.

Sammie will talk to me about anything but boys. Sometimes I think she just knows I might be a good role model for everything but relationships.

"She doesn't talk about it with anyone," Dylan once told me. "His name is Sullivan."

"First or last?" I ask.

He shrugs. "Does it matter? You didn't hear it from me."

Dylan continues with his story. "I sit with Natasha every day in the school cafeteria, and we go to her house and play sometimes, mostly board games. She's better than my last girlfriend, Annie, because she doesn't chase me around trying to kiss me all the time. I think she's the one."

"The one?" Robert and I both ask at the same time.

"Yeah, that I can eat lunch with for the rest of the school year."

Robert has a pained expression and is now standing, looking down at his Nike-soled feet. "Wanna tell us?" I ask.

"In a minute," he says, procrastinating as he flips through the channels to the college scores.

I had been there for both of my brothers' first loves and heartbreaks. I found ways of answering Eric's questions about what girls like without getting embarrassingly detailed and David's calls to ask whether it was okay to leave and come home to sleep with our dog instead of staying over the first time he had sex. I was there for their proms and their college breakups, when they each landed on my couch, ordering Chinese takeout. In between eating junk food and emptying six-packs of beers and sodas, they asked my advice, moping around until I made it clear they had to clean up the old food containers or get on with their lives. At that point they moved out.

Robert started to talk. "Her name is Jenna, and her birthday party is next week. She's a year younger than me. My present has to be the best one she gets."

"Why?" I asked, but already knew.

"Because she's awesome!"

"Tell me more about her."

"She's got really long dark brown hair, big green eyes and she loves jewelry."

"How do you know?" I asked the kid whose life revolved around Little League, the Knicks and Nintendo Wii.

"Because she's a girl," said Dylan, jumping in.

"Because she told me." Robert got very serious. I now knew who Jenna was. I met her once. She was walking past with two of her friends while Robert and I were playing basketball in the driveway. She waved, her arms jangling with bracelets. She came over to say hi, and I noticed her knack for accessorizing with shooting star stud earrings and a mix of wood and metal bangles and cuffs climbing up her arm.

Like most guys, my nephew seemed to be terrified of Jenna's affinity for bling and his inability to make the right choice. But he also knew it was a surefire way to win her heart.

Although I advise on the topic of jewelry as a career, I was still feeling honored that he came to me, until he said, "You wear the same things around your neck as she does," pointing to my layered pendants, and I had to wonder if I have the unique personal style of a ten-year-old.

I shrugged it off, happy that he chose me, not his dad, mom or his two aunts on my sister-in-law's side of his family. They might be better at getting married and sustaining relationships, but I am the go-to girl for making a good first impression. "You've got a great sense of style," Dylan said. "You definitely need to help Robert with the gift."

"Tell me a bit about her personality."

"She's smart, great at soccer, she's funny and she always laughs at my jokes," he offered. No laughing at my nephew's choice in jewelry, I thought, and planned out our trip to purchase Robert's first gift of love. Dylan was going to be in town until the weekend and wanted to come. I took them to a costume jewelry store in SoHo, a bit more unique than those at the mall yet still priced to accommodate his allowance. Pendants lined the walls; cocktail rings sat atop tables and bracelets were stacked high. Gliding his hand across a blackened skull with diamanté eyes, I shook my head no and indicated it was not really a gift that would represent affection. He let me know she was a bit of a tomboy and I shouldn't pick anything too "girly." I suggested a newer wood beaded bracelet with a dangling charm, which would work with the others she wore, but he wanted to keep looking around.

As we perused glittery dog tags and dangly earrings, I remembered back to the ghosts of my adolescent boyfriends past. After the ring debacle with Victor when I was the exact same age as Robert, I fell for Jeremy, who was my true love on and off from sixth to eighth grade. He made me a lanyard-style necklace in day camp during our second year together, which he figured gave him access to my breasts and after presenting it to me, proceeded immediately to try to feel me up. During one of our breakups early on in the eighth grade, I met Jeff, whom I spent an entire night into early morning making out with at a coed sleepover at a community center with little supervision. When I thought back about the laid-back attitude of grown-ups allowing us to share a sleeping bag all night long, my only conclusion was that it was the early seventies and no one quite knew what they were doing. Jeff professed his love for me by tying a macramé ankle bracelet with a single jade bead, which I was never supposed to take off. I felt safe with Jeff; he was a great kisser and would always call on time and make sure I got home all right. He was the only person I told that my parents were getting divorced, and then I decided he was too nice and broke up with him a month later. When he started smoking, hanging out with older boys from the next town over and giving one of my closest friends hickeys, I wanted him back.

In helping Robert, I had to wonder whether it was just me, or did all girls want just a taste of something we couldn't have, someone a bit dangerous to our hearts instead of nice boys accepting us and making us feel comfortable and cared for? Should I tell my nephew to play it a bit tougher, let the girls chase him? He'd already made up his mind that he loved Jenna wholeheartedly and wanted to show her without trepidation. He pointed out that she already wore a sterling silver peace sign, a wishbone, and a circle etched with her initials.

The boys told me they were starving, so we broke for lunch and headed over to Ben's, their favorite pizzeria on MacDougal Street in New York City. They wanted to talk to me about something else, and neither knew who should start the conversation.

"You guys can tell me anything," I explained, wiping the pizza oil dripping down Dylan's arm into his sleeve.

"Well," Robert started, taking a sip of his Sprite, "both of our dads are younger than you, but they got married first and had kids, and you never did."

"And we think it's a little weird," Dylan continued, handing me his crust.

"Okay, finish up. We really need to get back to the store before it closes," I said, trying to buy time to compose a suitable explanation that I myself didn't understand.

"It's just that we think you are prettier than any of our friends' mothers and you know the stuff you are supposed to know about, like, the best video games. You've watched all the Spider-Man movies with us and you're a great first baseman." Dylan was making his case.

"It just doesn't make sense," Robert added.

You're telling me, I thought, but didn't say.

"My mom says you pick the wrong men," Robert confided.

"Yeah, my dad says that too," Dylan piped in.

"This family is full of opinions, aren't they?" I tried to keep smiling at them.

"They just want to see you happy. We all want to see you happy." Dylan held the door to the store open for me as we walked back in.

"Why? Don't you guys think I am?"

"No"—Robert leaned in closely—"because the Italian boy couldn't commit."

I really needed to speak to my brothers and sisters-in-law about what they said in front of the kids.

"Do you know what commitment means?"

"Yeah, you wanted to marry him," Dylan offered.

"Maybe. But I have the two of you and Sammie, and that's enough for me."

I realized they were truly concerned about me. With Sammie, as much as she loved me, it was more contentious. The boys just loved and accepted me for who I was completely and without any judgment.

In a section with small 14K gold pendants, they picked out one in a heart shape with a tiny diamond above the word *hope*.

"This is a great choice for Jenna. I am sure she will love it." I was impressed at their taste and how they really didn't need me at all.

"No. This one's for you from the both of us," Robert explained.

I fought back the tears of pure joy welling up in my eyes and went in for the tight three-way hug I learned from my grandmother and mother. "Not now. When we get outside," Robert said.

In the end we got Jenna a wood beaded bracelet with three dangling charms. But I got the best gift of all: a pendant and—not one—but two guys to love and be happy with for the rest of my life.

CHAPTER 20

Pink Gold Rolex

*O*H GOD, ANOTHER VASE, I thought as Paolo handed me the artfully wrapped box with the most intricately woven Italian paper and muted ombre-shaded bow.

"How beautiful." I opened it and ran my hand down the sculptural shape and around the fluted texture of the Murano glass, set it down on my coffee table and hugged him as he sunk comfortably into my couch.

"I hope you like the color. It reminded me of"—he thought for a moment—"a deep violet sapphire stone." He said this with the satisfaction of someone who had just received a gemologist certificate.

After six tumultuous years with Paolo, four equally spectacular vases as gifts, twenty-five trips to Rome, countless transatlantic arguments, an equal amount of make-up sex and the past eleven months spent on hiatus from our relationship, I had been hoping for a gift that didn't simply evoke the *color* of a precious jewel. Perhaps a true sentimental token might have been more apropos to the occasion—the occasion being that Paolo and I had decided to give it another try and I'd invited him over to spend the Christmas through New Year's holiday week with me.

"I love the way you were able to fit this into your suitcase. It's amazing how you can carry on and pack your baggage with more stuff than anyone I know."

"Stop talking in metaphors." He pulled me closer, kissed my shoulder and unbuttoned my cashmere cardigan; a strap fell on my lace camisole. We hadn't seen each other for almost a year, and already my clothes were coming off. We were usually in bed, on the living room or bathroom floor, or one of our respective couches within twenty minutes of saying hello. I'd always wondered whether this was his way of normalizing things once we saw each other again or if he was just testing whether I was up for it and whether I wanted to be with him as much as the last time.

After all these months apart, I still did.

I was angry and miserable when I had left him in Italy eleven months earlier. After the flight landed at JFK from Rome and I'd made it through customs and baggage claim, I read the text that vibrated on my BlackBerry in the taxi, going to my apartment. Even though I cried, hated him and felt betrayed for ten hours during the flight home, I'd hoped there would be some message or e-mail.

Leaving my keys and my goddamn American checkbook on my bed with a note saying, "I think this is it" was just plain cowardly, it read. *You could have talked to me about it, said how you felt, but instead you let me come home to find this? I wasn't ready for this!* That was the crux of our problem. He never seemed prepared for me to walk away, but I was waiting for more: a sign, a message and a sentence that had the word *stay* in it.

I had talked to him many times about how I felt we were stagnant. Yet I allowed myself to hope that he would finally make good on his declarations of "I can't imagine life without you," which he had said many times. *Let's try being together in the same place* might have been a good start. The mixed messages and inconsistencies on his part had become too difficult to navigate; yet it took all my courage to leave him the way I had, without discussing it again. I didn't want to give him the chance to ask for more time. I deleted his message and put the BlackBerry back in my bag.

While we were apart, I realized the irony of my trying to gain distance. There were already five thousand miles and an ocean separating us. Yet, in the same way he had described the cuff links as an analogy for us, I felt attached and completely connected to him. I had known it would be difficult to break away, but I never realized until I did, how much we were part of each other's daily lives, that we were there to help each other through a rough day or week, depended on each other for security, to vent about our work, to be silly and know that neither of us was alone. "We have each other," he said whenever something went wrong and I was feeling sad or missing my mother.

During the first months that I stopped speaking to him, I immersed myself in work, got angry, wrote him e-mails I never sent, created diversions; I asked myself, *Why?* Why he couldn't he give me what I needed—a life with him—in the same city, country and postal code. I had nightmares about him and other women, asked all my friends, "Why?" I spread out on the couch and forgot to watch the movie I'd popped into the DVD; I asked my therapist, "Why?" I opened and shut the refrigerator door, forgetting what I'd gone to get, and even asked the refrigerator, "Why?"

But what I didn't do was write back, call or ask him.

After a month or so, he began to leave messages on my home phone, and I let Verizon's voice mail pick up: It could always be so much more aloof than me. I didn't answer his e-mails or his texts—the nonchalant questions or innocuous comments—trying to gauge how I felt or trying to keep communication going between us.

Hey, bella, sad that Updike died. What was his last book? The man ran an entire sales force for northern Italy. I was sure he'd heard of the Internet.

Hotter in Rome than usual. How about New York? Watch CNN.

Heard about the heightened security on the subway line. Take cabs until it's over. Thanks for the warning.

It went on. He began sending me quotes from books he thought I would like and a line or two reviewing a museum exhibit he saw.

I still didn't answer.

Instead, I quit smoking cold turkey and counted calories so I wouldn't gain weight from quitting smoking. I was in a constant haze of withdrawal symptoms: nicotine, sugar and inconsistent Italian men; I never knew which was the worst. I'd push myself out of bed each day, cry for two hours and exercise at the gym. Still I didn't answer him.

During that last visit to Rome, Paolo told me what hurt him most in our relationship was that each time I returned to New York after seeing him, I'd send him a short e-mail approximating the same sentiment: *I've had enough. I need to move on. I am saddened that we couldn't work it out, but you will always have a special place in my heart.*

"Maybe not every time, but it sure felt like it," he said. "I could never understand how you could just walk away so easily. A day earlier you are sitting across from me, laughing and hugging me, and then I am receiving an e-mail that leaves me abandoned and betrayed."

In my semicomatose, give-me-a-goddamn-cigarette state, I had moments of clarity. Writing good-bye when I got home was a way of protecting myself from the distance I felt was increasing. The night before I would leave him on each visit, he would find a way to push me away, starting irrational arguments or saying something cruel the night before we left each other. For me this felt final, as though we'd never be close again.

"You are scared of losing people. Didn't you realize that I am too? I couldn't deal with the emptiness of your not being there anymore. It was too sad to manage," he confessed. His self-awareness and inability to do anything about it always amazed me.

I realized I wrote the e-mails because I wanted it/him to change; I wanted more than he could give at the time. I also wanted to stick to what I said but at the same time hoped he wouldn't stay away for too long. He never did. But this time was different. I had grown tired of thinking something was wrong with me and trying to fix it because it was easier than fixing us. I was exhausted trying to work out all the nuances and complexities, the come-go, stay-leave dynamics of our relationship. I knew I still loved him and would miss him, but I had to try for a relationship closer to home that was simpler. Each month that went by seemed a lifetime away from him, and it took all the willpower I had to keep my distance.

Then a text message arrived, and in withdrawal speak, I fell off the wagon. *Do you believe how much I miss you, bella? Please, please speak to me! About anything!*

It was like catnip to the codependent, and I texted him back. *Call me when you want,* I typed, and hit SEND, skipping the twenty-four hours you are supposed to wait and mull it over. All that time I spent trying to separate from him was erased with one weak moment of feeling needed.

Two minutes later my home phone rang and did again each day after that. We fell back into talking every night, across time zones, and it took us only a week to find comfort in discussing our families, jobs and anything that was on our minds. We got our old routine back of having an argument, laughing about it quickly and having phone sex all within the same transatlantic phone call. When we talked about the holidays, I asked bluntly, "Why do you want to come?"

"Because I've waited so long to see you. I don't want to miss you anymore." And I invited him back into my life and to spend Christmas and New Year's with me.

And there he was, sitting on my couch and handing me a vase.

"You don't like it."

"No, it's beautiful," I said. "I'm trying to figure out where to put it." We surveyed the room.

"Did I buy you *all* of these?" Paolo asked.

"Yes." I nudged him with my foot. "You've always had great taste in glassware."

"I missed you." He kissed me in between my neck and my shoulder.

Paolo had great taste in leather, much like my father did.

Just as he would bring home beautiful belts for my mother after being in Italy at his textile mills, Paolo brought me a butter-soft lambskin three-quarter-length Bottega Veneta trench coat, a short suede denim-style Costume National jacket, a distressed structured-frame Prada bag and olive-and-aubergine-colored shearling gloves. He was generous; he knew my style and he knew designers. All that he had given me was elegant, and nothing seemed more personal than the "red vase that will look beautiful on the antique nightstand next to your bed."

And then a few days into our visit, I decided to torture myself and asked nonchalantly if he'd ever given a piece of jewelry to another woman.

"Well," he said, fidgeting with some euros in his pocket. "It wasn't a real piece of jewelry like the kind you wear," he admitted. "Okay, it was sterling silver and was more like art to wear."

"Stop using expressions I taught you." I was glaring but still ribbing him.

He took the change from his pocket and put it on the table. "It was Adriana's birthday, and I needed a gift. I was in a decorative store in Rome, which sold small sculptures by an artist who also made jewelry. The saleswoman knew so much about the artist, and she recommended this miniature of a human form. When the legs moved, well, you could see that he was a man." He continued, as usual, oblivious to how this was making me feel. "It was so cool, very tongue in cheek, and also beautifully made."

"Let me get this straight," I said. "Adriana, whom you met while we were on hiatus, was wearing, wait . . . a penis pendant around her neck that you got her, while you were texting that you missed *me*?"

"Did you forget that you were the one who left without a word and wouldn't speak to me for eleven months? You always change everything around. Stop acting like Anna Karenina."

"I am Russian. What do you expect?"

"Third generation. Give me a break. There is no reason for you to get all dramatic and dark."

"Did she like it?" I asked coolly, ready to smash the new vase over his head.

"Oh yes, and she wore it everywhere and got compliments from her friends. It was a real conversation piece."

This was one conversation I wanted to end, and although I was torn up that he'd bought another woman jewelry, a little badge that sort of made her his, I was, with all my heart and soul, glad that he hadn't bought this "art to wear" for me.

"It was cool," he reiterated.

"Probably best if you stop defending it now."

"*Bella*, how could I buy you jewelry?" he said without prompting. "It would be like buying a shirtmaker shirts."

"I would have liked something more personal than

Murano glass or gloves." I hated that I had just acted like a spoiled kid, but during our break from each other, I thought about how he'd never given me a piece of jewelry. It wasn't that I particularly needed a new bauble; it was what those tokens or lack thereof represented: romance and an expression of sentiment that no Prada handbag could offer.

"Hey, I bought you vibrators. Those were personal."

"Those were for you. It made you feel that I'd stay faithful when you were away."

"That's romantic!"

I walked out of the room. He followed me and then explained. "I tried. Really, I did. I stopped in stores in Rome, Milan and New York, but it's too scary buying you jewelry."

"Why?"

"Because you taught me about the different periods, the different cuts of diamonds, the different-colored stones and all their names; because you are picky and have very particular tastes."

He was with me when I tried on art deco brooches and when I found the perfect pair of diamond and ruby earrings. Once at a pawnshop on the outskirts of Trastevere, in Rome, I found a snake ring that was ancient with old mine cut diamond eyes, going for a price too good to resist. It had meaning; it was Italian like him. I collected antique serpent motifs, and he said it looked beautiful on me. I told the shopkeeper I would think about it, then took Paolo outside under the pretense of needing his advice.

"So, I think the price is great. It's in its original condition, and I love the way it slithers around my finger." He kept nodding his head.

"Go for it then. I really don't think you can go wrong."

I walked back in and bought it for myself. I noticed the moonstone cuff links with the sapphire bezels I had just had made for him on his shirt and tried to keep from having a major tantrum, the type I had when I was five. Next door was the Bottega Veneta shop where he wound up buying me the jacket, which was more costly and which I didn't love as much as the ring.

That night back in Milan, he tried to make it better; he took me out to my favorite restaurant and bought me the most beautiful flowers after dropping me off in front of his place when he went to park his car. He put on one of my favorite songs, the Doors' "Roadhouse Blues," and started to dance with me and then did a mock striptease, making me laugh and fall in love with him all over again like every time he did something goofy, vulnerable or sexy, or all three combined. Holding me in his arms before he fell asleep, he admitted he didn't know why he could not buy me the snake ring, except that it had connotations of more. "In the Italian tradition, you don't buy a woman a ring until you are ready to marry her."

I dropped it at the time because at that point in our relationship I wasn't thinking about marriage, but I never stopped wondering why he couldn't find a token of his affection, something small, something that would make me feel as cared for and special as he said my gifts of cuff links, hand-picked or designed expressly for him, made him feel.

During his stay in NYC, we went to MoMA and to see an Alvin Ailey ballet; we ate at Gotham, our favorite restaurant, watched old movies, stayed up talking and cuddled on my couch until I fell asleep. Then he carried me into the bedroom and helped me wriggle out of my clothes.

"We can't stay up the way we used to," he said, getting my arm caught in my turtleneck.

"And you're definitely not as smooth as you once were," I teased him.

He held me from behind, tickling my back. "At first I was just angry that you would leave like that," he whispered, "but as time went on, it got worse. The longer we didn't talk, I felt a part of me was missing. I couldn't concentrate at work, couldn't even get through a book. I'd read a couple of pages and not take anything in. I kept wondering what you were doing, where you were, who you were with and if you were thinking about me too."

"I was," I said softly, curling my body into his as tears trickled down from the corners of my eyes.

The days we were together; it felt natural, as though we hadn't spent all that time apart, except for the moments when he would ask me to never leave him again. Within the week, my heart was wide open. He listened to me on the phone with my niece and nephews. "I love the way you are with them and wish I could be as free with my feelings as you are," he said. He asked me to tell him more about my mother, knowing I missed her during the holidays, and said, "I really wish I had had the chance to meet her."

Paolo and I spent a night at the Pierre hotel, in a room overlooking his favorite view of Central Park. We went shopping for ties at Barneys and Bergdorf's; we joked when we came back to the room and counted them. I guessed that he had bought eleven.

"No way," he said. "How could you let me buy all of these? I am a shopaholic—is that how you say it?"

"Yep, that's how you say it." I sat on the bed, draping the ties around his neck. He pulled me down and we made love, fell asleep, took a shower together and went out for afternoon tea. I felt as though I had discovered New York and the two of us all over again. On Fifty-seventh between Park and Lexington, he spotted the Buccellati store and said, "Oh look—we have to go in."

Through my work, I'd learned about Buccellati (the multigenerational jewelry company born in Milan like Paolo), which dates back to an ancestor in the mid-eighteenth century. I had shown Paolo the intricately designed gems and rings first designed and handcrafted by Mario Buccellati when he opened the first shop under his name in 1919. Upon his death, his son Gianmaria (whom I had the pleasure of interviewing for a magazine profile story) took over the business and brought in his own son, Andrea. Both continue to work in the style and tradition of Mario, creating pieces that look like they are spun into golden lace and brocades and interwoven with small diamonds.

Many times at Sotheby's and Christie's, when the delicate rings went up at auction, I thought of bidding, but this was the one piece of jewelry I definitely wanted someone else to purchase for me. It was and still is my idea of the perfect wedding band. Paolo remembered how I admired them in Italy and led me into the Manhattan-based shop.

"So, which would you like to try on?" he asked. I selected almost everything in the display, not able to make a decision, and the sales associate took them out of the case, while Paolo slid them on my finger, one at a time, holding my hand up to the light while I pointed out that they were all handmade and hand engraved. "Your fingers are so long and aristocratic." He turned my hand one way and then the other. "Each one suits you so well," he said. "Do you have a favorite?"

I settled on two that I liked most. He placed one on my left hand and one on my right. "Wow, they both fit." The sales associate asked if we'd like some information on them. Paolo nodded his head yes. While we waited, he changed the subject and asked, "Hey, where is that great watch place we used to go to? Is it close?"

We left with stats and prices and photocopies; my heart sank as we headed out the door, but I didn't show it.

We arrived at Aaron Faber Gallery. The owner, Ed Faber, has been a friend for years and has sold me almost all my vintage men's watches, the only kind I will wear with the exception of my mother's art deco engagement watch and my father's Cartier Tank.

Ed had also provided Paolo, a novice collector, with a limited edition Hamilton's and a Jaeger-LeCoultre from the 1950s, both proud and handsome styles.

I zoomed in on a pink gold Rolex from the 1930s with an original dial, Mercedes hands and a brown leather strap. "Try it on." Ed, the consummate salesman, slid and buckled it around my wrist. I went to the mirror and saw that it suited me. I looked at the price, which didn't suit me, but I calculated that if I didn't buy the down coat I needed and that was on sale now, or the boots, and if I ate Cup-a-Soup for the rest of the winter, I just might be able to purchase it.

Paolo took my hand and said without hesitation, "I'd really like to buy this for you."

I was shocked. I was in love with the watch and, in that moment, deeply with him.

When we were back at my place, when the giddiness wore off, I realized this was the best Paolo could do. He couldn't get any closer than this.

That night, he continued to admire the Rolex on my wrist, but I couldn't help remembering the Buccellati on my finger.

The irony of time: I'd found a man very similar to my

dad. But I wanted more than a watch, more of a commitment than Paolo was willing to give. And, I knew, from the years I'd allowed our relationship to stay trapped in time, that he wouldn't be the one to say good-bye, but he also wouldn't change to give me the permanence or security I wanted in a relationship or a ring "that in the Italian tradition, a man buys only when he is ready to marry a woman."

CHAPTER 21

Buccellati Ring

"BIG BIRTHDAY COMING up." Sammie pointed this out as we both picked up the same tank top in Abercrombie. I quickly put it down.

"Nah. Forty-nine; no major deal. Just another day," I said, looking up from the rack and spotting my crow's-feet in the mirror, which seemed to have multiplied since the morning. Sammie imitated the faces I made and rolled her eyes at me.

"In Hollister, I can't see at all; I need a flashlight and a compact mirror to check out my rear in jeans. Here in Abercrombie, they have such harsh lighting that it makes me look gray. Maybe I shouldn't go shopping at 'your stores' anymore."

My niece laughed but continued to try to get me to discuss my age with her. I tried a new tack. "It's much more exciting for you. You're crossing over into your teenage years." I was amazed at how quickly she had gone from the adorable blond kid to the highlighted twelve-going-on-twenty bombshell; how she'd grown so quickly from the little girl who wanted Lady's necklace from the Disney classic to the young woman sporting diamond stud earrings and who went from reciting the ABCs to wearing a full C-cup bra.

Sammie didn't back down. "You're the one crossing over—and it's very big, five-oh big. The big five-oh. Forty plus ten; thirty plus twenty."

"Okay. Can you show off your math skills some other time?" I shushed her. She still didn't let up.

"It's 2009. You were born in 1959. And that adds up to . . . ?"

"Such a stickler for detail. Okay, Nancy Drew. I confess, but only you know."

She got the reference, thankfully, and I realized that besides her, only AJ, my grandmother and David's side of the family knew my real age. I had even started to believe it myself, and no one ever questioned it to my face, except for Sammie.

She dragged me into Claire's, which appeared to have taken on not only a retro look but had all the trappings of a seventies revival shop. "So nostalgic," I said. "Horrible hair, clothes that add ten pounds. Well, at least the jewelry was fun and, look—it's all here: peace signs, smiley faces, long beads and cameos on ribbon. I was the same age as you are now when this was all in style."

"You're making a comeback." She handed me a strand of puka shells.

Sure. Tell that to men my age, I thought but didn't say.

"Hey, why don't you throw a party? Something with a theme from when you and your friends were younger."

"That's an awful idea. Then everyone would find out."

"That's the whole point!" She rolled her eyes again.

Sammie has often given me some of the best advice. When boring Bill didn't call one weekend (which made him way less boring) while she was visiting, she said, "If you stop thinking about it, it will happen." Actually she only wanted me to concentrate on buying her boots; but she was right— the minute I was helping her decide on which style Uggs, he phoned. Another time, when I was leaving after a short visit, she said, "You are acting a bit quiet, kind of like the last time you left us. You are always really sad to say good-bye. But we will see you again soon." She threw her arms around me, she the adult and me the kid, trading roles, just as my mom and I had done all those years before.

"Hey, didn't your mom pretend she was younger when she met Grandpa Manny? Tell me the story again!"

I had told Sammie, Dylan and Robert the story the first time they were old enough to visit my mother at the cemetery. David had brought Sammie and Dylan in for spring break, and we all went—my brothers, my sisters-in-law, the kids and I. Neither my niece nor nephews ever had had the chance to meet my mother in person; they knew her only through photographs, old videos and the stories my brothers and I told them. They never got to know her as Grandma or Nana or any other term of endearment, but they loved hearing our tales about how we all got in trouble when we were young, the night I called the cops on her in the house in New City and other goofier times. When I saw them meeting her at her headstone for the first time, I had to walk away, unable to breathe or talk, my chest in a vise grip. David came and put his hand on my shoulder and told me, "Mom knows. She sees we are all here."

I pulled out a bag of charms from my handbag. I gave one to each of the kids, telling them, "We usually put rocks on the headstone to show we've been here and our love, but I think it would be more fun to leave tiny medallions." They all nodded their heads in agreement. Sammie placed a coin engraved with a daisy, my mother's favorite flower, which symbolizes happiness; Robert had a disk that spelled out the word *believe*; Dylan had a heart for love; I had one that said *Fide*—faith in Latin. "She will really love those," Sammie said, and held my hand in hers.

Once back at my house, I told them the story that Sammie had asked to hear again. My mother was thirty-seven and Manny was thirty-two when they met. She thought it was too much of an age difference, so she decided it was best to grow three years younger. She told David, Eric and me never to tell, under any circumstances. We thought she was a little wacky, but we agreed. Once when she had a kidney stone, she called me to get to the hospital first. I was happy to be there to hold her hand.

"I asked you to come here first because you're better with doctors and you can blacken out my age on the side of the bed. Please do it right now! Get a Sharpie from the nurses' station." Even while passing a kidney stone, she was able to tell me where to get the correct indelible pen.

It was by no means a master plan. Had Manny ever looked anywhere but at my mother while making sure she had ice chips and watching her IV, he might have been suspicious about the block of black ink that resided next to "Patient's Age."

When my mother passed away, Manny filled out the death certificate with the date of birth that she had told him. My grandmother and brothers and I knew it was wrong, yet we decided to leave it that way for the headstone, as a tribute to my mom and to signify that we had not told "under any circumstances."

"I love that story, but then something happened last year, right?" Sammie asked.

"Yes. Grandpa Manny turned sixty-five and put in for Social Security. He called me and said there was something wrong, because the Social Security office did not have a record with my mother's number and date of birth. It wasn't until a few hours later that it dawned on me. I called your dad and your uncle Eric and told them this was the one instance in which I would need to give Manny the correct information."

Manny immediately said, "Are you kidding? Your mother thought I would love her less if she were three years older? She was a nut." He loved her despite her age, her neurotic tendencies and for everything she was.

"See. It didn't change a thing," Sammie said.

Sammie was right. But for me, it finally did. My mother had provided me with perhaps the most important life lesson to date.

I would celebrate my age and everything else I had accomplished and not be afraid to be loved less or differently.

And when I got home, I sent an e-mail.

Dear Friends:

Something funny happened on the way to my turning forty-one. I forgot that I'd become forty-one the year before and celebrated the same birthday twice. (Celebrated might be pushing it.) There was something about being over forty that made me feel not just older but—how did my friendly neurologist put it? Oh yes, as if I were on borrowed time and everything might collapse at any second. Interestingly, you all believed it or maybe you just were kind enough to play along since I was only cheating by . . . one year.

My niece, a straight-A student in math and fortu-

nately a wise young soul, informed me that I was "cross-
ing over" and turning . . . fifty on November 5. Not
forty-nine, as I recently told my doctor, who, after giving
me my yearly physical, looked down at my chart and
then up at me as if I might be having signs of perimeno-
pausal memory loss or like I was pathological since I had
said it so convincingly. And yes, this is what fifty looks
like, for good, bad or indifferent. There is something about
seeing yourself in retrospect that offers new perspective.
Over forty was a mere blip. Hopefully, when I figure out
a time, all of you who live nearby will come for my
"coming out" party. I might even get with the brave new
world and learn how to send an Evite. Will keep you
posted. Thank you all for your understanding and keep-
ing any ageist comments to a minimum. If you haven't
already done so, you all will turn fifty one day.

I received a diverse array of responses, including from
newer friends saying this was nothing; they had lied by many
more years. One guy, whom I met on Match.com, dated and
then became friends with, said, "I got you beat. I said I was
forty-six but really am fifty-three." He surprised me; he
looked so good for his age, I'd thought I was dating a younger
man. AJ said, "Told you so." My old friends said they hadn't
noticed. Those I went to school with thought I'd skipped a
grade, not being able to remember many details about their
own younger selves. Nick told me it was a brilliant decep-

tion; he couldn't figure out why *he* felt older on *my* birthday every year, and now he realized that my becoming younger made him seem older.

I accidentally (okay, maybe on purpose) included Paolo on the contact list, and he immediately responded. *What? I had been seeing an older woman for six years and never knew it? I was aghast (correct word in English, bella?) . . . to find out via mass e-mail that I am five months younger rather than five months older than you!* And then he inserted two smiley faces.

Sammie was right. None of the people I knew cared about the year I misplaced for a while; what they did care about was me, and all wanted to help me celebrate.

I opted for seventies disco, dancing and ginger ale in a champagne glass for me, and I realized that it was okay. Sometime in the future I would be grappling with hot flashes, a countless number of wrinkles around my eyes and my once-swanlike neck would truly turn to chicken skin. Soon my ass would look like it belonged in a geriatric ward and my once-perky B-cups would be taken down by gravity no matter how many times I went to the gym. My stomach would develop another layer of padding no matter if I counted and ate fewer calories than when I had food poisoning. But I also knew that, as when I look at past photos today and ask, "Why did I see *only* my flaws?" I would not let that happen again.

I'd grown older, but I also had grown up and out of the defenses I had mastered to keep myself from getting too close or feeling too much loss. I'd been thrown into adulthood when I was young, but it had taken me until my forties to start coming of age and learning about myself.

The party was a success. Old loves—Ray and Nick had turned into two of my closest male friends—Celia, Jodi, my stepfather and a huge turnout of new and longtime friends all showed up. AJ, as always, was there. Even Paolo came to New York for the weekend of the party. We shared tender moments, he bought flowers—I was thankful they were not in a vase—and a plush cashmere sweater, and I accepted them for what they were. As he was leading me onto the dance floor, he noticed my hand and held it up to the light. He looked at it, then at me quizzically, confused, his face scrunched up the way it used to get when he was jealous of some other man. His grip tightening around my hand, he asked, "Who gave you the ring?" I was wearing my favorite of the Buccellati bands that he had asked me to try on the last time I had seen him.

During my twenties, I had started to choose rings I had wanted for my engagement, even when I wasn't with a specific guy. Maybe it was because I had missed out on playing with a ring when I was young, or maybe it was purely my love of something sparkly or that I had been more equipped to commit to a piece of jewelry than a man. I never went for the huge solitaire, but I had definitely wanted something romantic for my finger and not functional for my wrist. I had picked out a number of styles throughout the years, mostly antique: a double ruby and mine cut diamond heart ring with a crown from the 1860s, an engraved posy ring with a beautiful inscription in French, an intricately pierced art deco design with a mine cut center stone and tiny diamonds in the filigree work of the shank, and a five-stone Georgian-style ring with rose cut diamonds. My friend Raizel, the antiques dealer who taught me all I knew, thought it was interesting that although I was superstitious about many things, a ring pre-owned by a couple I didn't know had no effect on me.

I believed one good ultrasonic cleaning would wash away any remnants of a failed marriage. Sometimes we choose our superstitions based on what we fear. I had only two when it came to engagement or wedding rings. Raizel had acquired a beautiful large center rose cut diamond ring set in a white enameled band with an inscription engraved in gold, which I immediately had to try on. I was so excited. "If I had some-one to get engaged to, this would make a fabulous ring—so rare and very simple yet elegant. What does it mean?" I asked, always hungry for more jewelry history.

"It's a memorial ring."

"I thought they had black enameling?" I said.

"White too." She smiled at me, as if she knew exactly what I'd do next. "This one is for when the woman dies an unmarried virgin." I never got anything off my finger so fast and washed my hands immediately. Raizel and I laughed continuously for about ten minutes.

It reminded me of a time when I was nine and with my grandmother.

Nana Ida had taken me to an eclectic jewelry store in Brooklyn that had a diverse range of jewelry from the early twentieth century through the 1960s. When I asked to try on a wide silver band, a large formidable woman with a thick Russian accent came over and cautioned me, "Never wear anything on your left ring finger before someone proposes or you will never get married."

"We don't believe in old wives' tales," my grandmother said to her.

"We don't?" I quickly put down the ring. Then, during the next forty years of my life, I never wore anything on *that* finger.

"Are you going to answer me?" Paolo asked again, nervously. "Who gave you the ring?"

After I had scheduled the party, after he called to see if it was okay that he came, I was walking up Fifty-seventh Street when I realized I had learned to buy my own jewelry for years now, and I had purchased many other rings but never my absolute favorites. I had reserved them for the right guy at the right time. I decided to commemorate my big birthday by buying one of the Buccellati styles I had tried on all those months before. I walked into the shop and surveyed the cases filled with leaves and floral designs in the classic lace and honeycomb patterns. I chose a black rhodium-plated white gold ring with rose cut diamonds that looked like a delicate tulle fabric, and I wore it on my middle finger on my right hand. Maybe some things would never change. I would always be a tad superstitious. And, although I had listened to the Russian woman for forty-one years, I still hadn't gotten married, but . . . why play with fate?

I still didn't have the guy, nor did I have my own children. But I had two brothers who actually turned out to be "great to have as I got older" and kids in my life who made me feel like I belonged, whom I loved with all my heart and who loved me back and accepted me as their aunt, friend and confidante.

When both my parents died while I was in my thirties, I became an adult orphan and let it define me for a while. I took on too much and tried to fix everyone's lives instead of concentrating on working on my own. I realized that all the people and events over the course of my life so far had taught me how to love, stay put, be sad and finally move on when I needed to—and to grow. I would always grieve somewhere inside for my mother and my father and always a bit for what I wanted but didn't get. Yet I was tired of seeing mostly what was missing, when there was so much I did have. I still had my grandmother, and although moments of lucidity were becoming scarcer, she remembered me, and, at ninety-six, she still called me her "best friend." I had an extended family and a rich history and a hell of a lot to celebrate.

It was time to find the rainbows in the puddles on the ground again, like my mother had taught me when I was a kid, to smile when I saw a tiara on a young girl's head and to put on "a little lipstick," even when my heart was breaking.

I released my hand from Paolo's grip and told him to breathe. Then I explained I had bought the ring for myself. And I knew during that single moment that someday there would be the right guy with the left hand ring. But for now the Buccellati twinkling in the light represented all that I had accomplished and all the real gems and bright ornaments of love around me.

Acknowledgments

There are way too many people to thank in this project, but I really need to try to give them the credit for all their friendship, love, support and for putting up with me through this process.

To Samantha Taylor Bernstein, my niece, who will always be a fairy princess and the little girl in the twinkly tiara, and who adds the sparkle to my life.

Special thanks to: Susan Shapiro, for her constant guidance and limitless generosity; Lori Davis, for her friendship and endless readings; Britt Bivens, for her friendship and for kicking me in the butt to keep going; Nicole Robson, for her belief and enthusiasm about the project from the start; my aunt, Audrey Bernstein, for opening her home and windows; Michele Giulietti, for the "interesting" material he provided and for helping me to understand and sort it all out . . . and to my longest-time friend, Adam Judelson, for always, always being here and never "going/getting away."

To my brothers, David and Eric Bernstein, for letting me mine their memories and write about them without "being blackmailed for royalties"; to my sisters-in-law, Kim and Nadine, for helping to make me an aunt to the greatest kids I know; my nephews, Dylan Bernstein and Robert Bernstein, my two favorite guys, who have always made me feel "cool"; and my stepfather, Manny Bonazzo, for his support, long after he didn't "need" to give it anymore.

To Steven Van Patten and Lorne Jaffe, my good friends and great writers, for holding my hand and guiding me along when I thought I was messing up miserably. And to the other writer friends and teachers who taught me to push through the process, Toure, Jamie Cat Callan, Bruce Tracy and Devan Sipher.

To my editor, Danielle Perez, whose understanding, friendship, support, wisdom and brilliant editing gave this book its heart and soul; and to my agent, Ryan Fischer Harbage, thank you for taking me on and sticking it out with me!

To Todd Jackson, an incredible Web site designer, who had the patience to work on the process of creating my Web site and dealing with my strong opinions and my extremely limited technology vocabulary; and to Viviane Tubiana, my longtime friend and a graphic designer who helped me to realize what I wanted on this book and throughout my career.

I'd also like to thank Rosalind Parry, Julia Fleischaker, Jennifer Kamnitzer Schwabinger, and the many other people at NAL/Penguin for their time and effort.

This book also could not be possible without these long-time friends: the late and very great Jessica Marlowe Goldstein King (who brought great friends and the favorite parts of my youth back into my life—you will be my soul sister forever), Eileen Garrahan, Tony Cupo, Paul Provenza, Lee R. Schreiber, Denise Lipton Rothberg, Jodi Kaplan, Shelley Kaplan Saftler, Jayne Mountford, Sheryl Oliva, Rupert Howard, Jeff Volan, Vivian Koo, my stepmom, Lorraine Bernstein and my stepsister, Denise Propatier Maldonado.

And for my wonderful friends in the jewelry business, those I met through our joint love of this art, all major talents who taught and adorned me in knowledge, passion and, most important, support: the late Raizel Halpen, Edward Faber, Lorraine Wohl, Alice Kwartler, John Williams, Michael Khordipour, Oscar Silva, Patti Silva, Leo Smith, Janet Goldman, the late Jimmy Moore, Julie Lamb, Sam Koumi, the entire Toback family, Erica Courtney, Lorraine Depasque, Karen Alberg Grossman, Penny Preville, Jay Siskin, Warren Alberian, Mary Aulde, Sofia Kaman, Megan Thorne, Todd Reed, Ambrish Sethi, Pratima Sethi, Raffaella Mannelli, Alessio Mannelli, Moritz Glik, Lene Vibes Dahlgren, Shaill Jhaveri, Coomi Bhasin, Robin Rotenier, Jennifer Gandia, Jonathan Landsberg, Jeffrey Landsberg, Joanne Teichman, Marie Helene Morrow, Ellen Hertz, Julie

Ettinger, Lois Morgenstern, Paul Schneider, Jim Rosenheim, Lee Krombholtz, Helena Krodel, Lenny Kroll and Ashlee Moore of KC Designs, and Ron Saltiel and Bart Gorin of RSP Media.

And to my father, Melvin Gerald Bernstein, who is always in my heart.

About the Author

Beth Bernstein has written about dating, relationships and family for women's and lifestyle magazines, and has worked in the jewelry industry for twenty years. She runs her own consulting company, where she works with leading jewelry designers and retailers.

CONNECT ONLINE

beth-bernstein.com
bjeweled.wordpress.com
facebook.com/bethbernstein.ny
twitter.com/bethbjeweled